# THE TREASURY OF ANCIENT EGYPT

*TO*

*ALAN H. GARDINER, ESQ.,*

*M.A., D.LITT.*
*LAYCOCK STUDENT OF EGYPTOLOGY AT*
*WORCESTER COLLEGE, OXFORD,*

*THIS BOOK,*
*WHICH WILL RECALL SOME SUMMER NIGHTS*
*UPON THE THEBAN HILLS,*

*IS DEDICATED.*

# PREFACE.

No person who has travelled in Egypt will require to be told that it is a country in which a considerable amount of waiting and waste of time has to be endured. One makes an excursion by train to see some ruins, and, upon returning to the station, the train is found to be late, and an hour or more has to be dawdled away. Crossing the Nile in a rowing-boat the sailors contrive in one way or another to prolong the journey to a length of half an hour or more. The excursion steamer will run upon a sandbank, and will there remain fast for a part of the day.

The resident official, travelling from place to place, spends a great deal of time seated in railway stations or on the banks of the Nile, waiting for his train or his boat to arrive; and he has, therefore, a great deal of time for thinking. I often try to fill in these dreary periods by jotting down a few notes on some matter which has recently been discussed, or registering and elaborating arguments which have chanced lately to come into the thoughts. These notes are shaped and "written up" when next there is a spare hour, and a few books to refer to; and ultimately they take the form of articles or papers, some of which find their way into print.

This volume contains twelve chapters, written at various times and in various places, each dealing with some subject drawn from the great treasury of Ancient Egypt. Some of the chapters have appeared as articles in magazines. Chapters iv., v., and viii. were published in 'Blackwood's Magazine'; chapter vii. in 'Putnam's Magazine' and the 'Pall Mall Magazine'; and chapter ix. in the 'Century Magazine.' I have to thank the editors for allowing me to reprint them here. The remaining seven chapters have been written specially for this volume.

LUXOR, UPPER EGYPT,
*November* 1910.

# CONTENTS

## PART IV.—THE PRESERVATION OF THE TREASURY.

# ILLUSTRATIONS.

# PART I

## THE VALUE OF THE TREASURY.

"History no longer shall be a dull book. It shall walk incarnate in every just and wise man. You shall not tell me by languages and titles a catalogue of the volumes you have read. You shall make me feel what periods you have lived. A man shall be the Temple of Fame. He shall walk, as the poets have described that goddess, in a robe painted all over with wonderful events and experiences . . . He shall be the priest of Pan, and bring with him into humble cottages the blessing of the morning stars, and all the recorded benefits of heaven and earth."

EMERSON.

# CHAPTER I.

# THE VALUE OF ARCHÆOLOGY.

The archæologist whose business it is to bring to light by pick and spade the relics of bygone ages, is often accused of devoting his energies to work which is of no material profit to mankind at the present day. Archæology is an unapplied science, and, apart from its connection with what is called culture, the critic is inclined to judge it as a pleasant and worthless amusement. There is nothing, the critic tells us, of pertinent value to be learned from the Past which will be of use to the ordinary person of the present time; and, though the archæologist can offer acceptable information to the painter, to the theologian, to the philologist, and indeed to most of the followers of the arts and sciences, he has nothing to give to the ordinary layman.

In some directions the imputation is unanswerable; and when the interests of modern times clash with those of the past, as, for example, in Egypt where a beneficial reservoir has destroyed the remains of early days, there can be no question that the recording of the threatened information and the minimising of the destruction, is all that the value of the archæologist's work entitles him to ask for. The critic, however, usually overlooks some of the chief reasons that archæology can give for even this much consideration, reasons which constitute its modern usefulness; and I therefore propose to point out to him three or four of the many claims which it may make upon the attention of the layman.

In the first place it is necessary to define the meaning of the term "Archæology." Archæology is the study of the facts of ancient history and ancient lore. The word is applied to the study of all ancient documents and objects which may be classed as antiquities; and the archæologist is understood to be the man who deals with a period for which the evidence has to be excavated or otherwise discovered. The age at which an object becomes an antiquity, however, is quite undefined, though practically it may be reckoned at a hundred years; and ancient history is, after all, the tale of any period which is not modern. Thus an archæologist does not necessarily deal solely with the remote ages.

Every chronicler of the events of the less recent times who goes to the original documents for his facts, as true historians must do during at least a part of their studies, is an archæologist; and, conversely, every archæologist who in the course of his work states a series of historical facts, becomes an historian. Archæology and history are inseparable; and nothing is more detrimental to a noble science than the attitude of certain so-called archæologists who devote their entire time to the study of a sequence of objects without proper consideration for the history which those objects reveal. Antiquities are the relics of human mental energy; and they can no more be classified without reference to the minds which produced them than geological specimens can be discussed without regard to the earth. There is only one thing worse than the attitude of the archæologist who does not study the story of the periods with which he is dealing, or construct, if only in his thoughts, living history out of the objects discovered by him; and that is the attitude of the historian who has not familiarised himself with the actual relics left by the people of whom he writes, or has not, when possible, visited their lands. There are many "archæologists" who do not care a snap of the fingers for history, surprising as this may appear; and there are many historians who take no interest in manners and customs. The influence of either is pernicious.

It is to be understood, therefore, that in using the word Archæology I include History: I refer to history supplemented and aggrandised by the study of the arts, crafts, manners, and customs of the period under consideration.

As a first argument the value of archæology in providing a precedent for important occurrences may be considered. Archæology is the structure of ancient history, and it is the voice of history which tells us that a Cretan is always a Cretan, and a Jew always a Jew. History, then, may well take her place as a definite asset of statecraft, and the law of Precedent may be regarded as a fundamental factor in international politics. What has happened before may happen again; and it is the hand of the archæologist that directs our attention to the affairs and circumstances of olden times, and warns us of the possibilities of their recurrence. It may be said that the statesman who has ranged in the front of his mind the proven characteristics of the people with whom he is dealing has a perquisite of the utmost importance.

Any archæologist who, previous to the rise of Japan during the latter half of the nineteenth century, had made a close study of the history of that country and the character of its people, might well have predicted unerringly its future advance to the position of a first-class power. The amazing faculty of imitation displayed by the Japanese in old times was patent to him. He had seen them borrow part of their arts, their sciences, their crafts, their literature, their religion, and many of their customs from the Chinese; and he might have been aware that they would likewise borrow from the West, as soon as they had intercourse with it, those essentials of civilisation which would raise them to their present position in the world. To him their fearlessness, their tenacity, and their patriotism, were known; and he was so well aware of their powers of organisation, that he might have foreseen the rapid development which was to take place.

What historian who has read the ancient books of the Irish—the Book of the Dun Cow, the Book of Ballymote, the Book of Lismore, and the like—can show either surprise or dismay at the events which have occurred in Ireland in modern times? Of the hundreds of kings of Ireland whose histories are epitomised in such works as that of the old archæologist Keating, it would be possible to count upon the fingers those who have died in peace; and the archæologist, thus, knows better than to expect the descendants of these kings to live in harmony one with the other. National characteristics do not change unless, as in the case of the Greeks, the stock also changes.

In the Jews we have another example of the persistence of those national characteristics which history has made known to us. The Jews first appear in the dimness of the remote past as a group of nomad tribes, wandering over southern Palestine, Egypt, and the intervening deserts; and at the present day we see them still homeless, scattered over the face of the globe, the "tribe of the wandering foot and weary breast."

In no country has the archæologist been more active than in Egypt during the last half century, and the contributions which his spade and pick have offered to history are of first-rate importance to that study as a whole. The eye may now travel down the history of the Nile Valley from prehistoric days to the present time almost without interruption; and now that the anthropologist has shown that the modern Egyptians, Mussulman and Copt, peasant and townsman, belong to one and the same race of ancient Egyptians, one may surely judge today's inhabitants of the country in the light of yesterday's records. In his report for the year 1906, Lord Cromer, questioning whether the modern inhabitants of the country were capable of governing their own land, tells us that we must go back to the precedent of Pharaonic days to discover if the Egyptians ever ruled themselves successfully.

In this pregnant remark Lord Cromer was using information which the archæologist and historian had made accessible to him. Looking back over the history of the country, he was enabled, by the study of this information, to range before him the succession of foreign occupations of the Nile Valley and to assess their significance. It may be worth while to repeat the process, in order to give an example of the bearing of history upon modern polemics, though I propose to discuss this matter more fully in another chapter.

Previous to the British occupation the country was ruled, as it is now, by a noble dynasty of Albanian princes, whose founder was set upon the throne by the aid of Turkish and Albanian troops. From the beginning of the sixteenth century until that time Egypt had been ruled by the Ottoman Government, the Turk having replaced the Circassian and other foreign "Mamlukes" who had held the country by the aid of foreign troops since the middle of the thirteenth century. For a hundred years previous to the Mamluke rule Egypt had been in the hands of the Syrian and Arabian dynasty founded by Saladdin. The Fatimides, a North African dynasty, governed the country before the advent of Saladdin, this family having entered Egypt under their general, Jauhar, who was of Greek origin. In the ninth century Ahmed ibn Tulun, a Turk, governed the land with the aid of a foreign garrison, his rule being succeeded by the Ikhshidi dynasty of foreigners. Ahmed had captured Egypt from the Byzantines who had held it since the days of the Roman occupation. Previous to the Romans the Ptolemies, a Greek family, had governed the Nile Valley with the help of foreign troops. The Ptolemies had followed close upon the Greek occupation, the Greeks having replaced the Persians as rulers of Egypt. The Persian occupation had been preceded by an Egyptian dynasty which had been kept on the throne by Greek and other foreign garrisons. Previous to this there had been a Persian occupation, which had followed a short period of native rule under foreign influence. We then come back to the Assyrian conquest which had followed the Ethiopian rule. Libyan kings had held the country before the Ethiopian conquest. The XXIst and XXth Dynasties preceded the Libyans, and here, in a disgraceful period of corrupt government, a series of so-called native kings are met with. Foreigners, however, swarmed in the country at the time, foreign troops were constantly used, and the Pharaohs themselves were of semi-foreign origin. One now comes back to the early XIXth and XVIIIth Dynasties which, although largely tinged with foreign blood, may be said to have been Egyptian families. Before the rise of the XVIIIth Dynasty the country was in foreign hands for the long period which had followed the fall of the XIIth Dynasty, the classical period of Egyptian history (about the twentieth century B.C.), when there were no rivals to be feared. Thus the Egyptians may be said to have been subject to foreign occupation for nearly four thousand years, with the exception of the strong native rule of the XVIIIth Dynasty, the semi-native rule of the three succeeding dynasties, and a few brief periods of chaotic government in later times; and this is the information which the archæologist has to give to the statesman and politician. It is a story of continual conquest, of foreign occupations following one upon another, of revolts and massacres, of rapid retributions and punishments. It is the story of a nation which, however ably it may govern itself in the future, has only once in four thousand years successfully done so in the past.

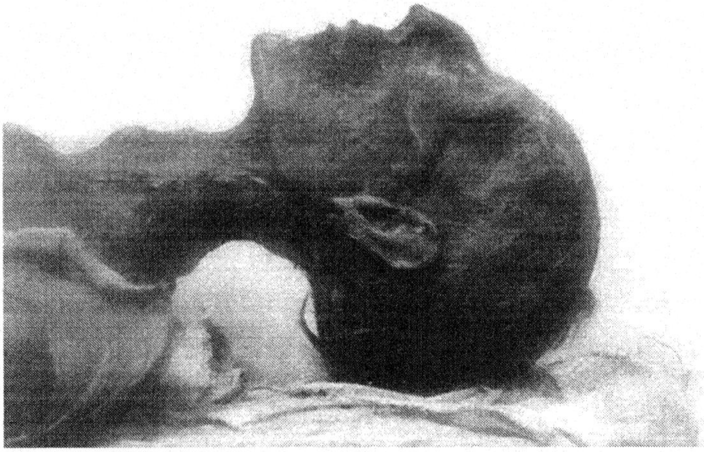

PL. I. The mummy of Rameses II. of Dynasty XIX.
—CAIRO MUSEUM.
*[Photo by E. Brugsch Pasha.*

Such information is of far-reaching value to the politician, and to those interested, as every Englishman should be, in Imperial politics. A nation cannot alter by one jot or tittle its fundamental characteristics; and only those who have studied those characteristics in the pages of history are competent to foresee the future. A certain Englishman once asked the Khedive Ismail whether there was any news that day about Egyptian affairs. "That is so like all you English," replied his Highness. "You are always expecting something new to happen in Egypt day by day. Today is here the same as yesterday, and tomorrow will be the same as today; and so it has been, and so it will be, for thousands of years."[1] Neither Egypt nor any other nation will ever change; and to this it is the archæologist who will bear witness with his stern law of Precedent.

I will reserve the enlarging of this subject for the next chapter: for the present we may consider, as a second argument, the efficacy of the past as a tonic to the present, and its ability to restore the vitality of any age that is weakened.

In ancient Egypt at the beginning of the XXVIth Dynasty (B.C. 663) the country was at a very low ebb. Devastated by conquests, its people humiliated, its government impoverished, a general collapse of the nation was imminent. At this critical period the Egyptians turned their minds to the glorious days of old. They remodelled their arts and crafts upon those of the classical periods, introduced again the obsolete offices and titles of those early times, and organised the government upon the old lines. This movement saved the country, and averted its collapse for a few more centuries. It renewed the pride of workmanship in a decadent people; and on all sides we see a revival which was the direct result of an archæological experiment.

The importance of archæology as a reviver of artistic and industrial culture will be realised at once if the essential part it played in the great Italian Renaissance is called to mind. Previous to the age of Cimabue

---

1 E. Dicey. 'The Story of the Khedivate,' p. 528.

and Giotto in Florence, Italian refinement had passed steadily down the path of deterioration. Græco-Roman art, which still at a high level in the early centuries of the Christian era, entirely lost its originality during Byzantine times, and the dark ages settled down upon Italy in almost every walk of life. The Venetians, for example, were satisfied with comparatively the poorest works of art imported from Constantinople or Mount Athos: and in Florence so great was the poverty of genius that when Cimabue in the thirteenth century painted that famous Madonna which to our eyes appears to be of the crudest workmanship, the little advance made by it in the direction of naturalness was received by the city with acclamations, the very street down which it was carried being called the "Happy Street" in honour of the event. Giotto carried on his master's teachings, and a few years later the Florentines had advanced to the standard of Fra Angelico, who was immediately followed by the two Lippis and Botticelli. Leonardo da Vinci, artist, architect, and engineer, was almost contemporaneous with Botticelli, being born not much more than a hundred years after the death of Giotto. With him art reached a level which it has never surpassed, old traditions and old canons were revived, and in every direction culture proceeded again to those heights from which it had fallen.

The reader will not need to be reminded that this great renaissance was the direct result of the study of the remains of the ancient arts of Greece and Rome. Botticelli and his contemporaries were, in a sense, archæologists, for their work was inspired by the relics of ancient days.

Now, though at first sight it seems incredible that such an age of barbarism as that of the later Byzantine period should return, it is indeed quite possible that a relatively uncultured age should come upon us in the future; and there is every likelihood of certain communities passing over to the ranks of the absolute Philistines. Socialism run mad would have no more time to give to the intellect than it had during the French Revolution. Any form of violent social upheaval means catalepsy of the arts and crafts, and a trampling under foot of old traditions. The invasions and revolts which are met with at the close of ancient Egyptian history brought the culture of that country to the lowest ebb of vitality. The fall of Greece put an absolute stop to the artistic life of that nation. The invasions of Italy by the inhabitants of less refined countries caused a set-back in civilisation for which almost the whole of Europe suffered. Certain of the French arts and crafts have never recovered from the effects of the Revolution.

A national convulsion of one kind or another is to be expected by every country; and history tells us that such a convulsion is generally followed by an age of industrial and artistic coma, which is brought to an end not so much by the introduction of foreign ideas as by a renascence of the early traditions of the nation. It thus behoves every man to interest himself in the continuity of these traditions, and to see that they are so impressed upon the mind that they shall survive all upheavals, or with ease be re-established.

There is no better tonic for a people who have weakened, and whose arts, crafts, and industries have deteriorated than a return to the conditions which obtained at a past age of national prosperity; and there are few more repaying tasks in the long-run than that of reviving an interest in the best periods of artistic or industrial activity. This can only be effected by the study of the past, that is to say by archæology.

It is to be remembered, of course, that the sentimental interest in antique objects which, in recent years, has given a huge value to all ancient things, regardless of their intrinsic worth, is a dangerous attitude, unless it is backed by the most expert knowledge; for instead of directing the attention only to the best work of the best periods, it results in the diminishing of the output of modern original work and the setting of little of worth in its place. A person of a certain fashionable set will now boast that there is no object in his room less than two hundred years old: his only boast, however, should be that the room contains nothing which is not of intrinsic beauty, interest, or good workmanship. The old chairs from the kitchen are dragged into the drawing-room—because they are old; miniatures unmeritoriously painted by unknown artists for obscure clients are nailed in conspicuous places—because they are old; hideous plates and dishes, originally made by ignorant workmen for impoverished peasants, are enclosed in glass cases—because they are old; iron-bound chests, which had been cheaply made to suit the purses of farmers, are rescued from the cottages of their descendants and sold for fabulous sums—because they are old.

A person who fills a drawing-room with chairs, tables, and ornaments, dating from the reign of Queen Anne, cannot say that he does so because he wishes it to look like a room of that date; for if this were his desire, he would have to furnish it with objects which appeared to be newly made, since in the days of Queen Anne the first quality noticeable in them would have been their newness. In fact, to produce the desired effect everything in the room, with very few exceptions, would have to be a replica. To sit in this room full of antiques in a frock-coat would be as bad a breach of good taste as the placing of a Victorian chandelier in an Elizabethan banqueting-hall. To furnish the room with genuine antiquities because they are old and therefore interesting would be to carry the museum spirit into daily life with its attending responsibilities, and would involve all manner of incongruities and inconsistencies; while to furnish in this manner because antiques were valuable would be merely vulgar. There are, thus, only three justifications that I can see for the action of the man who surrounds himself with antiquities: he must do so because they are examples of workmanship, because they are beautiful, or because they are endeared to him by family usage. These, of course, are full and complete justifications; and the value of his attitude should be felt in the impetus which it gives to conscientious modern work. There are periods in history at which certain arts, crafts, or industries reached an extremely high level of excellence; and nothing can be more valuable to modern workmen than familiarity with these periods. Well-made replicas have a value that is overlooked only by the inartistic. Nor must it be forgotten that modern objects of modern design will one day become antiquities;

and it should be our desire to assist in the making of the period of our lifetime an age to which future generations will look back for guidance and teaching. Every man can, in this manner, be of use to a nation, if only by learning to reject poor work wherever he comes upon it—work which he feels would not stand against the criticism of Time; and thus it may be said that archæology, which directs him to the best works of the ancients, and sets him a standard and criterion, should be an essential part of his education.

PL. II Wood and enamel jewel-case discovered in the tomb of Yuaa and Tuau. An example of the furniture of one of the best periods of ancient Egyptian art.—CAIRO MUSEUM.

*[Photo by E. Brugsch Pasha.*

The third argument which I wish to employ here to demonstrate the value of the study of archæology and history to the layman is based upon the assumption that patriotism is a desirable ingredient in a man's character. This is a premise which assuredly will be admitted. True patriotism is essential to the maintenance of a nation. It has taken the place, among certain people, of loyalty to the sovereign; for the armies which used to go to war out of a blind loyalty to their king, now do so from a sense of patriotism which is shared by the monarch (if they happen to have the good fortune to possess one).

Patriotism is often believed to consist of a love of one's country, in an affection for the familiar villages or cities, fields or streets, of one's own dwelling-place. This is a grievous error. Patriotism should be an unqualified desire for the welfare of the race as a whole. It is not really patriotic for the Englishman to say, "I love England": it is only natural. It is not patriotic for him to say, "I don't think much of foreigners": it is only a form of narrowness of mind which, in the case of England and certain other countries, happens sometimes to be rather a useful attitude, but in the case of several nations, of which a good example is Egypt, would be detrimental to their own interests. It was not unqualified patriotism that induced the Greeks to throw off the Ottoman yoke: it was largely dislike of the Turks. It is not patriotism, that is to say undiluted concern for the nation as a whole, which leads some of the modern Egyptians to prefer an entirely native government to the Anglo-Egyptian administration now obtaining in that country: it is restlessness; and I am fortunately able to define it thus without the necessity of entering the arena of polemics by an opinion as to whether that restlessness is justified or not justified.

If patriotism were but the love of one's tribe and one's dwelling-place, then such undeveloped or fallen races as, for example, the American Indians, could lay their downfall at the door of that sentiment; since the exclusive love of the tribe prevented the small bodies from amalgamating into one great nation for the opposing of the invader. If patriotism were but the desire for government without interference, then the breaking up of the world's empires would be urged, and such federations as the United States of America would be intolerable.

Patriotism is, and must be, the desire for the progress and welfare of the whole nation, without any regard whatsoever to the conditions under which that progress takes place, and without any prejudice in favour either of self-government or of outside control. I have no hesitation in saying that the patriotic Pole is he who is in favour of Russian or German control of his country's affairs; for history has told him quite plainly that he cannot manage them himself. The Nationalist in any country runs the risk of being the poorest patriot in the land, for his continuous cry is for self-government, without any regard to the question as to whether such government will be beneficial to his nation in the long-run.

The value of history to patriotism, then, is to be assessed under two headings. In the first place, history defines the attitude which the patriot should assume. It tells him, in the clear light of experience, what is, and what is not, good for his nation, and indicates to him how much he may claim for his country. And in the second place, it gives to the patriots of those nations which have shown capacity and ability in the past a confidence in the present; it permits in them the indulgence of that enthusiasm which will carry them, sure-footed, along the path of glory.

Archæology, as the discovery and classification of the facts of history, is the means by which we may obtain a true knowledge of what has happened in the past. It is the instrument with which we may dissect legend, and extract from myth its ingredients of fact. Cold history tells the Greek patriot, eager to enter the fray, that he must set little store by the precedent of the deeds of the Trojan war. It tells the English patriot that the "one jolly Englishman" of the old rhyme is not the easy vanquisher of the "two froggy Frenchmen and one Portugee" which tradition would have him believe. He is thus enabled to steer a middle course between arrant conceit and childish fright. History tells him the actual facts: history is to the patriot what "form" is to the racing man.

In the case of the English (Heaven be praised!) history opens up a boundless vista for the patriotic. The Englishman seldom realises how much he has to be proud of in his history, or how loudly the past cries upon him to be of good cheer. One hears much nowadays of England's peril, and it is good that the red signals of danger should sometimes be displayed. But let every Englishman remember that history can tell him of greater perils faced successfully; of mighty armies commanded by the greatest generals the world has ever known, held in check year after year, and finally crushed by England; of vast fleets scattered or destroyed by English sailors; of almost impregnable cities captured by British troops. "There is something very characteristic," writes Professor Seeley,[1] "in the indifference which we show towards the mighty phenomenon of the diffusion of our race and the expansion of our state. We seem, as it were, to have conquered and peopled half the world in a fit of absence of mind."

The history of England, and later of the British Empire, constitutes a tale so amazing that he who has the welfare of the nation as a whole at heart—that is to say, the true patriot—is justified in entertaining the most optimistic thoughts for the future. He should not be indifferent to the past: he should bear it in mind all the time. Patriotism may not often be otherwise than misguided if no study of history has been made. The patriot of one nation will wish to procure for his country a freedom which history would show him to have been its very curse; and the patriot of another nation will encourage a nervousness and restraint in his people which history would tell him was unnecessary. The English patriot has a history to read which, at the present time, it is especially needful for him to consider; and, since Egyptology is my particular province, I cannot better close this argument than

1 'The Expansion of England,' p. 10.

by reminding the modern Egyptians that their own history of four thousand years and its teaching must be considered by them when they speak of patriotism. A nation so talented as the descendants of the Pharaohs, so industrious, so smart and clever, should give a far larger part of its attention to the arts, crafts, and industries, of which Egyptian archæology has to tell so splendid a story.

As a final argument for the value of the study of history and archæology an aspect of the question may be placed before the reader which will perhaps be regarded as fanciful, but which, in all sincerity, I believe to be sober sense.

In this life of ours which, under modern conditions, is lived at so great a speed, there is a growing need for a periodical pause wherein the mind may adjust the relationship of the things that have been to those that are. So rapidly are our impressions received and assimilated, so individually are they shaped or classified, that, in whatever direction our brains lead us, we are speedily carried beyond that province of thought which is common to us all. A man who lives alone finds himself, in a few months, out of touch with the thought of his contemporaries; and, similarly, a man who lives in what is called an up-to-date manner soon finds himself grown unsympathetic to the sober movement of the world's slow roundabout.

Now, the man who lives alone presently developes some of the recognised eccentricities of the recluse, which, on his return to society, cause him to be regarded as a maniac; and the man who lives entirely in the present cannot argue that the characteristics which he has developed are less maniacal because they are shared by his associates. Rapidly he, too, has become eccentric; and just as the solitary man must needs come into the company of his fellows if he would retain a healthy mind, so the man who lives in the present must allow himself occasional intercourse with the past if he would keep his balance.

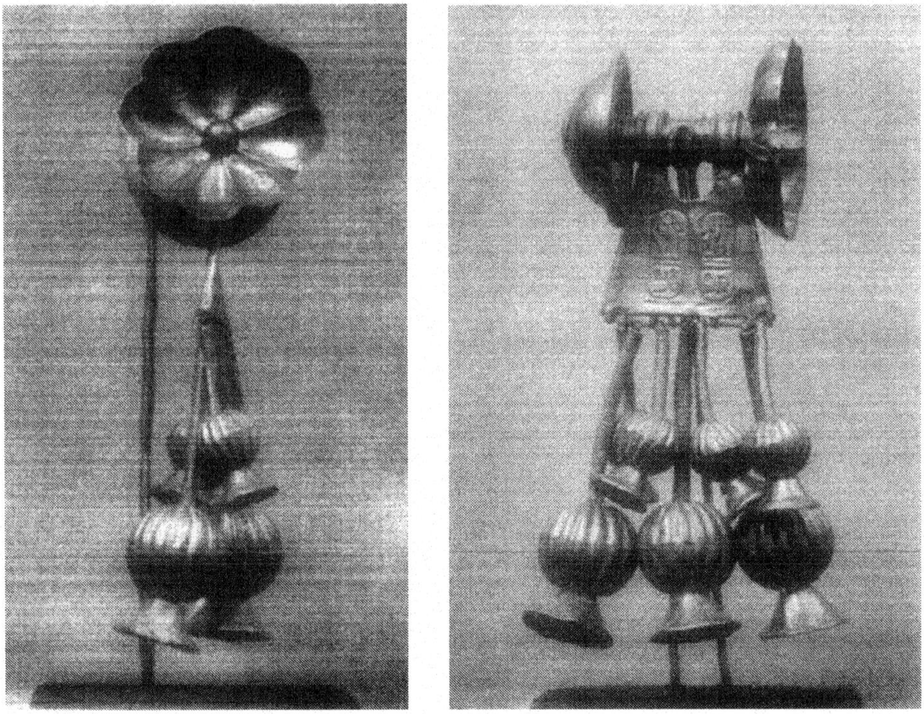

PL. III. Heavy gold earrings of Queen Tausert of Dynasty XX. An example of the work of ancient Egyptian goldsmiths.—CAIRO MUSEUM.]

*[Photo by E. Brugsch Pasha.*

Heraclitus, in a quotation preserved by Sextus Empiricus,[1] writes: "It behoves us to follow the common reason of the world; yet, though there is a common reason in the world, the majority live as though they possessed a wisdom peculiar each unto himself alone." Every one of us who considers his mentality an important part of his constitution should endeavour to give himself ample opportunities of adjusting his mind

1 Bywater: 'Heracliti Ephesii Reliquiæ,' p. 38.

to this "common reason" which is the silver thread that runs unbroken throughout history. We should remember the yesterdays, that we may know what the pother of today is about; and we should foretell tomorrow not by today but by every day that has been.

Forgetfulness is so common a human failing. In our rapid transit through life we are so inclined to forget the past stages of the journey. All things pass by and are swallowed up in a moment of time. Experiences crowd upon us; the events of our life occur, are recorded by our busy brains, are digested, and are forgotten before the substance of which they were made has resolved into its elements. We race through the years, and our progress is headlong through the days.

Everything, as it is done with, is swept up into the basket of the past, and the busy handmaids, unless we check them, toss the contents, good and bad, on to the great rubbish heap of the world's waste. Loves, hates, gains, losses, all things upon which we do not lay fierce and strong hands, are gathered into nothingness, and, with a few exceptions, are utterly forgotten.

And we, too, will soon have passed, and our little brains which have forgotten so much will be forgotten. We shall be throttled out of the world and pressed by the clumsy hands of Death into the mould of that same rubbish-hill of oblivion, unless there be a stronger hand to save us. We shall be cast aside, and left behind by the hurrying crowd, unless there be those who will see to it that our soul, like that of John Brown, goes marching along. There is only one human force stronger than death, and that force is History, By it the dead are made to live again: history is the salvation of the mortal man as religion is the salvation of his immortal life.

Sometimes, then, in our race from day to day it is necessary to stop the headlong progress of experience, and, for an hour, to look back upon the past. Often, before we remember to direct our mind to it, that past is already blurred, and dim. The picture is out of focus, and turning from it in sorrow instantly the flight of our time begins again. This should not be. "There is," says Emerson, "a relationship between the hours of our life and the centuries of time." Let us give history and archæology its due attention; for thus not only shall we be rendering a service to all the dead, not only shall we be giving a reason and a usefulness to their lives, but we shall also lend to our own thought a balance which in no otherwise can be obtained, we shall adjust ourselves to the true movement of the world, and, above all, we shall learn how best to serve that nation to which it is our inestimable privilege to belong.

# CHAPTER II.

## THE EGYPTIAN EMPIRE.

"History," says Sir J. Seeley, "lies before science as a mass of materials out of which a political doctrine can be deduced . . . Politics are vulgar when they are not liberalised by history, and history fades into mere literature when it loses sight of its relation to practical politics . . . Politics and history are only different aspects of the same study."[1]

These words, spoken by a great historian, form the keynote of a book which has run into nearly twenty editions; and they may therefore be regarded as having some weight. Yet what historian of old Egyptian affairs concerns himself with the present welfare and future prospects of the country, or how many statesmen in Egypt give close attention to a study of the past? To the former the Egypt of modern times offers no scope for his erudition, and gives him no opportunity of making "discoveries," which is all he cares about. To the latter, Egyptology appears to be but a pleasant amusement, the main value of which is the finding of pretty scarabs suitable for the necklaces of one's lady friends. Neither the one nor the other would for a moment admit that Egyptology and Egyptian politics "are only different aspects of the same study." And yet there can be no doubt that they are.

It will be argued that the historian of ancient Egypt deals with a period so extremely remote that it can have no bearing upon the conditions of modern times, when the inhabitants of Egypt have altered their language,

1 'The Expansion of England.'

religion, and customs, and the Mediterranean has ceased to be the active centre of the civilised world. But it is to be remembered that the study of Egyptology carries one down to the Muhammedan invasion without much straining of the term, and merges then into the study of the Arabic period at so many points that no real termination can be given to the science; while the fact of the remoteness of its beginnings but serves to give it a greater value, since the vista before the eyes is wider.

It is my object in this chapter to show that the ancient history of Egypt has a real bearing on certain aspects of the polemics of the country. I need not again touch upon the matters which were referred to on page 8 in order to demonstrate this fact. I will take but one subject—namely, that of Egypt's foreign relations and her wars in other lands. It will be best, for this purpose, to show first of all that the ancient and modern Egyptians are one and the same people; and, secondly, that the political conditions, broadly speaking, are much the same now as they have been throughout history.

Professor Elliot Smith, F.R.S., has shown clearly enough, from the study of bones of all ages, that the ancient and modern inhabitants of the Nile Valley are precisely the same people anthropologically; and this fact at once sets the matter upon an unique footing: for, with the possible exception of China, there is no nation in the world which can be proved thus to have retained its type for so long a period. This one fact makes any parallel with Greece or Rome impossible. The modern Greeks have not much in common, anthropologically, with the ancient Greeks, for the blood has become very mixed; the Italians are not the same as the old Romans; the English are the result of a comparatively recent conglomeration of types. But in Egypt the subjects of archaic Pharaohs, it seems certain, were exactly similar to those of the modern Khedives, and new blood has never been introduced into the nation to an appreciable extent, not even by the Arabs. Thus, if there is any importance in the bearing of history upon politics, we have in Egypt a better chance of appreciating it than we have in the case of any other country.

It is true that the language has altered, but this is not a matter of first-rate importance. A Jew is not less typical because he speaks German, French, or English; and the cracking of skulls in Ireland is introduced as easily in English as it was in Erse. The old language of the Egyptian hieroglyphs actually is not yet quite dead; for, in its Coptic form, it is still spoken by many Christian Egyptians, who will salute their friends in that tongue, or bid them good-morning or goodnight. Ancient Egyptian in this form is read in the Coptic churches; and God is called upon by that same name which was given to Amon and his colleagues. Many old Egyptian words have crept into the Arabic language, and are now in common use in the country; while often the old words are confused with Arabic words of similar sound. Thus, at Abydos, the archaic fortress is now called the *Shunet es Zebib*, which in Arabic would have the inexplicable meaning "the store-house of raisins"; but in the old Egyptian language its name, of similar sound, meant "the fortress of the Ibis-jars," several of these sacred birds having been buried there in jars, after the place had been disused as a military stronghold. A large number of Egyptian towns still bear their hieroglyphical names: Aswan, (Kom) Ombo, Edfu, Esneh, Keft, Kus, Keneh, Dendereh, for example. The real origin of these being now forgotten, some of them have been given false Arabic derivations, and stories have been invented to account for the peculiar significance of the words thus introduced. The word *Silsileh* in Arabic means "a chain," and a place in Upper Egypt which bears that name is now said to be so called because a certain king here stretched a chain across the river to interrupt the shipping; but in reality the name is derived from a mispronounced hieroglyphical word meaning "a boundary." Similarly the town of Damanhur in Lower Egypt is said to be the place at which a great massacre took place, for in Arabic the name may be interpreted as meaning "rivers of blood," whereas actually the name in Ancient Egyptian means simply "the Town of Horus." The archæological traveller in Egypt meets with instances of the continued use of the language of the Pharaohs at every turn; and there are few things that make the science of

Egyptology more alive, or remove it further from the dusty atmosphere of the museum, than this hearing of the old words actually spoken by the modern inhabitants of the land.

The religion of Ancient Egypt, like those of Greece and Rome, was killed by Christianity, which largely gave place, at a later date, to Muhammedanism; and yet, in the hearts of the people there are still an extraordinary number of the old pagan beliefs. I will mention a few instances, taking them at random from my memory.

In, ancient days the ithiphallic god Min was the patron of the crops, who watched over the growth of the grain. In modern times a degenerate figure of this god Min, made of whitewashed wood and mud, may be seen standing, like a scarecrow, in the fields throughout Egypt. When the sailors cross the Nile they may often be heard singing *Ya Amuni, Ya Amuni*, "O Amon, O Amon," as though calling upon that forgotten god for assistance. At Aswan those who are about to travel far still go up to pray at the site of the travellers' shrine, which was dedicated to the gods of the cataracts. At Thebes the women climb a certain hill to make their supplications at the now lost sanctuary of Meretsegert, the serpent-goddess of olden times. A snake, the relic of the household goddess, is often kept as a kind of pet in the houses of the peasants. Barren women still go to the ruined temples of the forsaken gods in the hope that there is virtue in the stones; and I myself have given permission to disappointed husbands to take their childless wives to these places, where they have kissed the stones and embraced the figures of the gods. The hair of the jackal is burnt in the presence of dying people, even of the upper classes, unknowingly to avert the jackal-god Anubis, the Lord of Death. A scarab representing the god of creation is sometimes placed in the bath of a young married woman to give virtue to the water. A decoration in white paint over the doorways of certain houses in the south is a relic of the religious custom of placing a bucranium there to avert evil. Certain temple-watchmen still call upon the spirits resident in the sanctuaries to depart before they will enter the building. At Karnak a statue of the goddess Sekhmet is regarded with holy awe; and the goddess who once was said to have massacred mankind is even now thought to delight in slaughter. The golden barque of Amon-Ra, which once floated upon the sacred lake of Karnak, is said to be seen sometimes by the natives at the present time, who have not yet forgotten its former existence. In the processional festival of Abu'l Haggag, the patron saint of Luxor, whose mosque and tomb stand upon the ruins of the Temple of Amon, a boat is dragged over the ground in unwitting remembrance of the dragging of the boat of Amon in the processions of that god. Similarly in the *Mouled el Nebi* procession at Luxor, boats placed upon carts are drawn through the streets, just as one may see them in the ancient paintings and reliefs. The patron gods of Kom Ombo, Horur and Sebek, yet remain in the memories of the peasants of the neighbourhood as the two brothers who lived in the temple in the days of old. A robber entering a tomb will smash the eyes of the figures of the gods and deceased persons represented therein, that they may not observe his actions, just as did his ancestors four thousand years ago. At Gurneh a farmer recently broke the arms of an ancient statue, which lay half-buried near his fields, because he believed that they had damaged his crops. In the south of Egypt a pot of water is placed upon the graves of the dead, that their ghost, or *ka*, as it would have been called in old times, may not suffer from thirst; and the living will sometimes call upon the name of the dead, standing at night in the cemeteries.

The ancient magic of Egypt is still widely practised, and many of the formulæ used in modern times are familiar to the Egyptologist. The Egyptian, indeed, lives in a world much influenced by magic and thickly populated by spirits, demons, and djins. Educated men holding Government appointments, and dressing in the smartest European manner, will describe their miraculous adventures and their meetings with djins. An Egyptian gentleman holding an important administrative post, told me the other day how his cousin was wont to change himself into a cat at night time, and to prowl about the town. When a boy, his father noticed this peculiarity, and on one occasion chased and beat the cat, with the result that the boy's body next morning was found to be covered with stripes and bruises. The uncle of my informant once read such strong language (magically) in a certain book that it began to tremble violently, and finally made a dash for it out of the window. This same personage was once sitting beneath a palm-tree with a certain magician (who, I fear, was also a conjurer), when, happening to remark on the clusters of dates twenty feet or so above his head, his friend stretched his arms upwards and his hands were immediately filled with the fruit. At another time this magician left his overcoat by mistake in a railway carriage, and only remembered it when the train was a mere speck upon the horizon; but, on the utterance of certain words, the coat immediately flew through the air back to him.

I mention these particular instances because they were told to me by educated persons; but amongst the peasants even more incredible stories are gravely accepted. The Omdeh, or headman, of the village of Chaghb, not far from Luxor, submitted an official complaint to the police a short time ago against an *afrit* or devil which was doing much mischief to him and his neighbours, snatching up oil-lamps and pouring the oil over the terrified villagers, throwing stones at passers-by, and so forth. Spirits of the dead in like manner haunt the living, and often do them mischief. At Luxor, lately, the ghost of a well-known robber persecuted his widow to such an extent that she finally went mad. A remarkable parallel to this case, dating from Pharaonic days, may be mentioned. It is the letter of a haunted widower to his dead wife, in which he asks her why she persecutes him, since he was always kind to her during her life, nursed her through illnesses, and never grieved her heart.[1]

These instances might be multiplied, but those which I have quoted will serve to show that the old gods are still alive, and that the famous

1 Maspero: 'Études egyptologiques,' i. 145.

magic of the Egyptians is not yet a thing of the past. Let us now turn to the affairs of everyday life.

An archæological traveller in Egypt cannot fail to observe the similarity between old and modern customs as he rides through the villages and across the fields. The houses, when not built upon the European plan, are surprisingly like those of ancient days. The old cornice still survives, and the rows of dried palm stems, from which its form was originally derived, are still to be seen on the walls of gardens and courtyards. The huts or shelters of dried corn-stalks, so often erected in the fields, are precisely the same as those used in prehistoric days; and the archaic bunches of corn-stalks smeared with mud, which gave their form to later stone columns, are set up to this day, though their stone posterity are now in ruins. Looking through the doorway of one of these ancient houses, the traveller, perhaps, sees a woman grinding corn or kneading bread in exactly the same manner as her ancestress did in the days of the Pharaohs. Only the other day a native asked to be allowed to purchase from us some of the ancient millstones lying in one of the Theban temples, in order to re-use them on his farm. The traveller will notice, in some shady corner, the village barber shaving the heads and faces of his patrons, just as he is seen in the Theban tomb-paintings of thousands of years ago; and the small boys who scamper across the road will have just the same tufts of hair left for decoration on their shaven heads as had the boys of ancient Thebes and Memphis. In another house, where a death has occurred, the mourning women, waving the same blue cloth which was the token of mourning in ancient days, will toss their arms about in gestures familiar to every student of ancient scenes. Presently the funeral will issue forth, and the men will sing that solemn yet cheery tune which never fails to call to mind the far-famed *Maneros*—that song which Herodotus describes as a plaintive funeral dirge, and which Plutarch asserts was suited at the same time to festive occasions. In some other house a marriage will be taking place, and the singers and pipers will, in like manner, recall the scenes upon the monuments. The former have a favourite gesture—the placing of the hand behind the ear as they sing—which is frequently shown in ancient representations of such festive scenes. The dancing girls, too, are here to be seen, their eyes and cheeks heavily painted, as were those of their ancestresses; and in their hands are the same tambourines as are carried by their class in Pharaonic paintings and reliefs. The same date-wine which intoxicated the worshippers of the Egyptian Bacchus goes the round of this village company, and the same food stuff, the same small, flat loaves of bread, are eaten.

Passing out into the fields the traveller observes the ground raked into the small squares for irrigation which the prehistoric farmer made; and the plough is shaped as it always was. The *shadoof*, or water-hoist, is patiently worked as it has been for thousands of years; while the cylindrical hoist employed in Lower Egypt was invented and introduced in Ptolemaic times. Threshing and winnowing proceed in the manner represented on the monuments, and the methods of sowing and reaping have not changed. Along the embanked roads, men, cattle, and donkeys file past against the sky-line, recalling the straight rows of such figures depicted so often upon the monuments. Overhead there flies the vulture goddess Nekheb, and the hawk Horus hovers near by. Across the road ahead slinks the jackal, Anubis; under one's feet crawls Khepera, the scarab; and there, under the sacred tree, sleeps the horned ram of Amon. In all directions the hieroglyphs of the ancient Egyptians pass to and fro, as though some old temple-inscription had come to life. The letter *m*, the owl, goes hooting past. The letter *a*, the eagle, circles overhead; the sign *ur*, the wagtail, flits at the roadside, chirping at the sign *rekh*, the peewit. Along the road comes the sign *ab*, the frolicking calf; and near it is *ka*, the bull; while behind them walks the sign *fa*, a man carrying a basket on his head. In all directions are the figures from which the ancients made their hieroglyphical script; and thus that wonderful old writing at once ceases to be mysterious, a thing of long ago, and one realises how natural a product of the country it was.

PL. IV. In the palm-groves near Sakkâra, Egypt.
*[Photo by E. Bird.*

In a word, ancient and modern Egyptians are fundamentally similar. Nor is there any great difference to be observed between the country's relations with foreign powers in ancient days and those of the last hundred years. As has been seen in the last chapter, Egypt was usually occupied by a foreign power, or ruled by a foreign dynasty, just as at the present day; and a foreign army was retained in the country during most of the later periods of ancient history. There were always numerous foreigners settled in Egypt, and in Ptolemaic and Roman times Alexandria and Memphis swarmed with them. The great powers of the civilised world were always watching Egypt as they do now, not always in a friendly attitude to that one of themselves which occupied the country; and the chief power with which Egypt was concerned in the time of the Ramesside Pharaohs inhabited Asia Minor and perhaps Turkey, just as in the middle ages and the last century. Then, as in modern times, Egypt had much of her attention held by the Sudan, and constant expeditions had to be made into the regions above the cataracts. Thus it cannot be argued that ancient history offers no precedent for modern affairs because all things have now changed. Things have changed extremely little, broadly speaking; and general lines of conduct have the same significance at the present time as they had in the past.

I wish now to give an outline of Egypt's relationship to her most important neighbour, Syria, in order that the bearing of history upon modern political matters may be demonstrated; for it would seem that the records of the past make clear a tendency which is now somewhat overlooked. I employ this subject simply as an example.

From the earliest historical times the Egyptians have endeavoured to hold Syria and Palestine as a vassal state. One of the first Pharaohs with whom we meet in Egyptian history, King Zeser of Dynasty III., is known to have sent a fleet to the Lebanon in order to procure cedar wood, and there is some evidence to show that he held sway over this country. For how many centuries previous to his reign the Pharaohs had overrun Syria we cannot now say, but there is no reason to suppose that Zeser initiated the aggressive policy of Egypt in Asia. Sahura, a Pharaoh of Dynasty V., attacked the Phoenician coast with his fleet, and returned to the Nile Valley with a number of Syrian captives. Pepi I. of the succeeding dynasty also attacked the coast-cities, and Pepi II. had considerable intercourse with Asia. Amenemhat I., of Dynasty XII., fought in Syria, and appears to have brought it once more under Egyptian sway. Senusert I. seems to have controlled the country to some extent, for Egyptians lived there in some numbers. Senusert III. won a great victory over the Asiatics in Syria; and a stela and statue belonging to Egyptian officials have been found at Gezer, between Jerusalem and the sea. After each of the above-mentioned wars it is to be presumed that the Egyptians held Syria for some years, though little is now known of the events of these far-off times.

During the Hyksos dynasties in Egypt there lived a Pharaoh named Khyan who was of Semitic extraction; and there is some reason to suppose that he ruled from Baghdad to the Sudan, he and his fathers having created a great Egyptian Empire by the aid of foreign troops. Egypt's connection with Asia during the Hyksos rule is not clearly defined, but the very fact that these foreign kings were anxious to call themselves "Pharaohs" shows that Egypt dominated in the east end of the Mediterranean. The Hyksos kings of Egypt very probably held Syria in fee, being possessed of both countries, but preferring to hold their court in Egypt.

We now come to the great Dynasty XVIII., and we learn more fully of the Egyptian invasions of Syria. Ahmosis I. drove the Hyksos out of the Delta and pursued them through Judah. His successor, Amenhotep I., appears to have seized all the country as far as the Euphrates; and Thutmosis I., his son, was able to boast that he ruled even unto that river. Thutmosis III., Egypt's greatest Pharaoh, led invasion after invasion into Syria, so that his name for generations was a terror to the inhabitants. From the Euphrates to the fourth cataract of the Nile the countries acknowledged him king, and the mighty Egyptian fleet patrolled the seas. This Pharaoh fought no less than seventeen campaigns in Asia, and he left to his son the most powerful throne in the world. Amenhotep II. maintained this empire and quelled the revolts of the Asiatics with a strong hand. Thutmosis IV., his son, conducted two expeditions into Syria; and the next king, Amenhotep III., was acknowledged throughout that country.

That extraordinary dreamer, Akhnaton, the succeeding Pharaoh, allowed the empire to pass from him owing to his religious objections to war; but, after his death, Tutankhamen once more led the Egyptian armies into Asia. Horemheb also made a bid for Syria; and Seti I. recovered Palestine. Rameses II., his son, penetrated to North Syria; but, having come into contact with the new power of the Hittites, he was unable to hold the country. The new Pharaoh, Merenptah, seized Canaan and laid waste the land of Israel. A few years later, Rameses III. led his fleet and his army to the Syrian coast and defeated the Asiatics in a great sea-battle. He failed to hold the country, however, and after his death Egypt remained impotent for two centuries. Then, under Sheshonk I., of Dynasty XXII., a new attempt was made, and Jerusalem was captured. Takeloth II., of the same dynasty, sent thither an Egyptian army to help in the overthrow of Shalmaneser II.

From this time onwards the power of Egypt had so much declined that the invasions into Syria of necessity became more rare. Shabaka of Dynasty XXV. concerned himself deeply with Asiatic politics, and attempted to bring about a state of affairs which would have given him the opportunity of seizing the country. Pharaoh Necho, of the succeeding dynasty, invaded Palestine and advanced towards the Euphrates. He recovered for Egypt her Syrian province, but it was speedily lost again. Apries, a few years later, captured the Phoenician coast and invaded Palestine; but the country did not remain for long under Egyptian rule. It is not necessary to record all the Syrian wars of the Dynasty of the Ptolemies. Egypt and Asia were now closely connected, and at several periods during this phase of Egyptian history the Asiatic province came under the control of the Pharaohs. The wars of Ptolemy I. in Syria were conducted on a large scale. In the reign of Ptolemy III. there were three campaigns, and I cannot refrain from quoting a contemporary record of the King's powers if only for the splendour of its wording:—

"The great King Ptolemy . . . having inherited from his father the royalty of Egypt and Libya and Syria and Phoenicia and Cyprus and Lycia and Caria and the Cyclades, set out on a campaign into Asia with infantry and cavalry forces, a naval armament and elephants, both Troglodyte and Ethiopic . . . But having become master of all the country within the Euphrates, and of Cilicia and Pamphylia and Ionia and the Hellespont and Thrace, and of all the military forces and elephants in these countries, and having made the monarchs in all these places his subjects, he crossed the Euphrates, and having brought under him Mesopotamia and Babylonia and Susiana and Persis and Media, and all the rest as far as Bactriana . . . he sent forces through the canals—" (Here the text breaks off.)

Later in this dynasty Ptolemy VII. was crowned King of Syria, but the kingdom did not remain long in his power. Then came the Romans, and for many years Syria and Egypt were sister provinces of one empire.

There is no necessity to record the close connection between the two countries in Arabic times. For a large part of that era Egypt and Syria formed part of the same empire; and we constantly find Egyptians fighting in Asia. Now, under Edh Dhahir Bebars of the Baharide Mameluke Dynasty, we see them helping to subject Syria and Armenia; now, under El-Mansur Kalaun, Damascus is captured; and now En Nasir Muhammed is found reigning from Tunis to Baghdad. In the Circassian Mameluke Dynasty we see El Muayyad crushing a revolt in Syria, and El Ashraf Bursbey capturing King John of Cyprus and keeping his hand on Syria. And so the tale continues, until, as a final picture, we see Ibrahim Pasha leading the Egyptians into Asia and crushing the Turks at Iconium.

Such is the long list of the wars waged by Egypt in Syria. Are we to suppose that these continuous incursions into Asia have suddenly come to an end? Are we to imagine that because there has been a respite for a hundred years the precedent of six thousand years has now to be disregarded? By the recent reconquest of the Sudan it has been shown that the old political necessities still exist for Egypt in the south, impelling her to be mistress of the upper reaches of the Nile. Is there now no longer any chance of her expanding in other directions should her hands become free?

The reader may answer with the argument that in early days England made invasion after invasion into France, yet ceased after a while to do so. But this is no parallel. England was impelled to war with France because the English monarchs believed themselves to be, by inheritance, kings of a large part of France; and when they ceased to believe this they ceased to make war. The Pharaohs of Egypt never considered themselves to be kings of Syria, and never used any title suggesting an inherited sovereignty.

They merely held Syria as a buffer state, and claimed no more than an overlordship there. Now Syria is still a buffer state, and the root of the trouble, therefore, still exists. Though I must disclaim all knowledge of modern politics, I am quite sure that it is no meaningless phrase to say that England will most carefully hold this tendency in check prevent an incursion into Syria; but, with a strong controlling hand relaxed, it would require more than human strength to eradicate an Egyptian tendency—nay, a habit, of six thousand years' standing. Try as she might, Egypt, as far as an historian can see, would not be able to prevent herself passing ultimately into Syria again. How or when this would take place an Egyptologist cannot see, for he is accustomed to deal in long periods of time, and to consider the centuries as others might the decades. It might not come for a hundred years or more: it might come suddenly quite by accident.

In 1907 there was a brief moment when Egypt appeared to be, quite unknowingly, on the verge of an attempted reconquest of her lost province. There was a misunderstanding with Turkey regarding the delineation of the Syrio-Sinaitic frontier; and, immediately, the Egyptian Government took strong action and insisted that the question should be settled. Had there been bloodshed the seat of hostilities would have been Syria; and supposing that Egypt had been victorious, she would have pushed the opposing forces over the North Syrian frontier into Asia Minor, and when peace was declared she would have found herself dictating terms from a point of vantage three hundred miles north of Jerusalem. Can it be supposed that she would then have desired to abandon the reconquered territory?

However, matters were settled satisfactorily with the Porte, and the Egyptian Government, which had never realised this trend of events, and had absolutely no designs upon Syria, gave no further consideration to Asiatic affairs. In the eyes of the modern onlookers the whole matter had developed from a series of chances; but in the view of the historian the moment of its occurrence was the only chance about it, the *fact* of its occurrence being inevitable according to the time-proven rules of history. The phrase "England in Egypt" has been given such prominence of late that a far more important phrase, "Egypt in Asia," has been overlooked. Yet, whereas the former is a catch-word of barely thirty years' standing, the latter has been familiar at the east end of the Mediterranean for forty momentous centuries at the lowest computation, and rings in the ears of the Egyptologist all through the ages. I need thus no justification for recalling it in these pages.

Now let us glance at Egypt's north-western frontier. Behind the deserts which spread to the west of the Delta lies the oasis of Siwa; and from here there is a continuous line of communication with Tripoli and Tunis. Thus, during the present winter (1910-11), the outbreak of cholera at Tripoli has necessitated the despatch of quarantine officials to the oasis in order to prevent the spread of the disease into Egypt. Now, of late years we have heard much talk regarding the Senussi fraternity, a Muhammedan sect which is said to be prepared to declare a holy war and to descend upon Egypt. In 1909 the Egyptian Mamur of Siwa was murdered, and it was freely stated that this act of violence was the beginning of the trouble. I have no idea as to the real extent of the danger, nor do I know whether this bogie of the west, which is beginning to cause such anxiety in Egypt in certain classes, is but a creation of the imagination; but it will be interesting to notice the frequent occurrence of hostilities in this direction, since the history of Egypt's gateways is surely a study meet for her guardians.

When the curtain first rises upon archaic times, we find those far-off Pharaohs struggling with the Libyans who had penetrated into the Delta from Tripoli and elsewhere. In early dynastic history they are the chief enemies of the Egyptians, and great armies have to be levied to drive them back through Siwa to their homes. Again in Dynasty XII., Amenemhat I. had to despatch his son to drive these people out of Egypt; and at the beginning of Dynasty XVIII., Amenhotep I. was obliged once more to give them battle. Seti I. of Dynasty XIX. made war upon them, and repulsed their invasion into Egypt. Rameses II. had to face an alliance of Libyans, Lycians, and others, in the western Delta. His son Merenptah waged a most desperate war with them in order to defend Egypt against their incursions, a war which has been described as the most perilous in Egyptian history; and it was only after a battle in which nine thousand of the enemy were slain that the war came to an end. Rameses III., however, was again confronted with these persistent invaders, and only succeeded in checking them temporarily. Presently the tables were turned, and Dynasty XXII., which reigned so gloriously in Egypt, was Libyan in origin. No attempt was made thenceforth for many years to check the peaceful entrance of Libyans into Egypt, and soon that nation held a large part of the Delta. Occasional mention is made of troubles upon the north-west frontier, but little more is heard of any serious invasions. In Arabic times disturbances are not infrequent, and certain sovereigns, as for example, El Mansur Kalaun, were obliged to invade the enemy's country, thus extending Egypt's power as far as Tunis.

There is one lesson which may be learnt from the above facts—namely, that this frontier is somewhat exposed, and that incursions from North Africa by way of Siwa are historic possibilities. If the Senussi invasion of Egypt is ever attempted it will not, at any rate, be without precedent.

When England entered Egypt in 1882 she found a nation without external interests, a country too impoverished and weak to think of aught else but its own sad condition. The reviving of this much-bled, anæmic people, and the reorganisation of the Government, occupied the whole attention of the Anglo-Egyptian officials, and placed Egypt before their eyes in only this one aspect. Egypt appeared to be but the Nile Valley and the Delta; and, in truth, that was, and still is, quite as much as the hard-worked officials could well administer. The one task of the regeneration of Egypt was all absorbing, and the country came to be regarded as a little land wherein a concise, clearly-defined, and compact problem could be worked out.

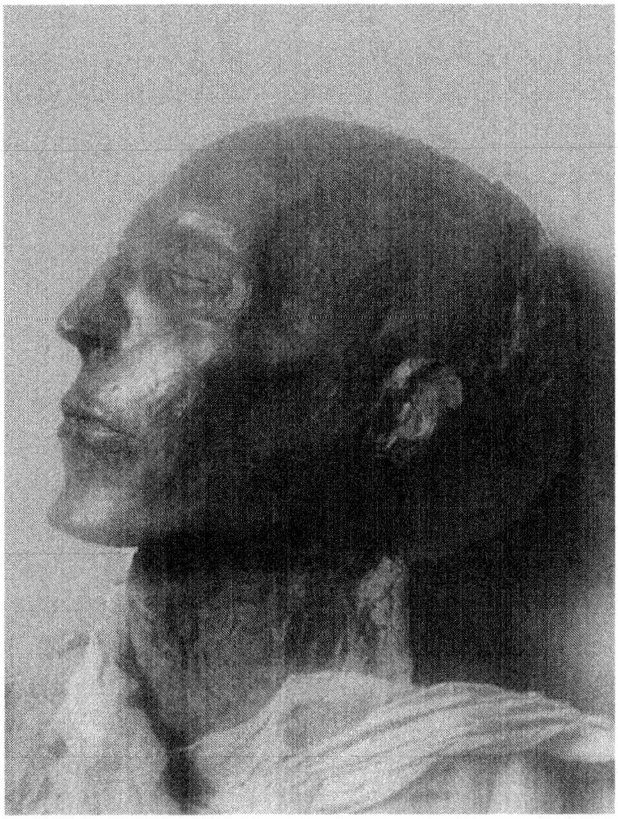

PL. V. The mummy of Sety I. of Dynasty XIX.
—CAIRO MUSEUM.
*[Photo by E. Brugsch Pasha.*

Now, while this was most certainly the correct manner in which to face the question, and while Egypt has benefited enormously by this singleness of purpose in her officials, it was, historically, a false attitude. Egypt is not a little country: Egypt is a crippled Empire. Throughout her history she has been the powerful rival of the people of Asia Minor. At one time she was mistress of the Sudan, Somaliland, Palestine, Syria,

Libya, and Cyprus; and the Sicilians, Sardinians, Cretans, and even Greeks, stood in fear of the Pharaoh. In Arabic times she held Tunis and Tripoli, and even in the last century she was the foremost Power at the east end of the Mediterranean. Napoleon when he came to Egypt realised this very thoroughly, and openly aimed to make her once more a mighty empire. But in 1882 such fine dreams were not to be considered: there was too much work to be done in the Nile Valley itself. The Egyptian Empire was forgotten, and Egypt was regarded as permanently a little country. The conditions which we found here we took to be permanent conditions. They were not. We arrived when the country was in a most unnatural state as regards its foreign relations; and we were obliged to regard that state as chronic. This, though wise, was absolutely incorrect. Egypt in the past never has been for more than a short period a single country; and all history goes to show that she will not always be single in the future.

With the temporary loss of the Syrian province Egypt's need for a navy ceased to exist; and the fact that she is really a naval power has now passed from men's memory. Yet it was not much more than a century ago that Muhammed Ali fought a great naval battle with the Turks, and utterly defeated them. In ancient history the Egyptian navy was the terror of the Mediterranean, and her ships policed the east coast of Africa. In prehistoric times the Nile boats were built, it would seem, upon a seafaring plan: a fact that has led some scholars to suppose that the land was entered and colonised from across the waters. We talk of Englishmen as being born to the sea, as having a natural and inherited tendency towards "business upon great waters"; and yet the English navy dates from the days of Queen Elizabeth. It is true that the Plantagenet wars with France checked what was perhaps already a nautical bias, and that had it not been for the Norman conquest, England, perchance would have become a sea power at an earlier date. But at best the tendency is only a thousand years old. In Egypt it is seven or eight thousand years old at the lowest computation. It makes one smile to think of Egypt as a naval power. It is the business of the historian to refrain from smiling, and to remark only that, absurd as it may sound, Egypt's future is largely upon the water as her past has been. It must be remembered that she was fighting great battles in huge warships three or four hundred feet in length at a time when Britons were paddling about in canoes.

One of the ships built by the Pharaoh Ptolemy Philopator was four hundred and twenty feet long, and had several banks of oars. It was rowed by four thousand sailors, while four hundred others managed the sails. Three thousand soldiers were also carried upon its decks. The royal dahabiyeh which this Pharaoh used upon the Nile was three hundred and thirty feet long, and was fitted with state rooms and private rooms of considerable size. Another vessel contained, besides the ordinary cabins, large bath-rooms, a library, and an astronomical observatory. It had eight towers, in which there were machines capable of hurling stones weighing three hundred pounds or more, and arrows eighteen feet in length. These huge vessels were built some two centuries before Cæsar landed in Britain.[1]

In conclusion, then, it must be repeated that the present Nile-centred policy in Egypt, though infinitely best for the country at this juncture, is an artificial one, unnatural to the nation except as a passing phase; and what may be called the Imperial policy is absolutely certain to take its place in time, although the Anglo-Egyptian Government, so long as it exists, will do all in its power to check it. History tells us over and over again that Syria is the natural dependant of Egypt, fought for or bargained for with the neighbouring countries to the north; that the Sudan is likewise a natural vassal which from time to time revolts and has to be reconquered; and that Egypt's most exposed frontier lies on the north-west. In conquering the Sudan at the end of the nineteenth century the Egyptians were but fulfilling their destiny: it was a mere accident that their arms were directed against a Mahdi. In discussing seriously the situation in the western oases, they are working upon the precise rules laid down

1 Athenæus, v. 8.

by history. And if their attention is not turned in the far future to Syria, they will be defying rules even more precise, and, in the opinion of those who have the whole course of Egyptian history spread before them, will but be kicking against the pricks. Here surely we have an example of the value of the study of a nation's history, which is not more nor less than a study of its political tendencies.

Speaking of the relationship of history to politics, Sir J. Seeley wrote: "I tell you that when you study English history, you study not the past of England only but her future. It is the welfare of your country, it is your whole interest as citizens, that is in question when you study history." These words hold good when we deal with Egyptian history, and it is our business to learn the political lessons which the Egyptologist can teach us, rather than to listen to his dissertations upon scarabs and blue glaze. Like the astronomers of old, the Egyptologist studies, as it were, the stars, and reads the future in them; but it is not the fashion for kings to wait upon his pronouncements any more! Indeed he reckons in such very long periods of time, and makes startling statements about events which probably will not occur for very many years to come, that the statesman, intent upon his task, has some reason to declare that the study of past ages does not assist him to deal with urgent affairs. Nevertheless, in all seriousness, the Egyptologist's study is to be considered as but another aspect of statecraft, and he fails in his labours if he does not make this his point of view.

In his arrogant manner the Egyptologist will remark that modern politics are of too fleeting a nature to interest him. In answer, I would tell him that if he sits studying his papyri and his mummies without regard for the fact that he is dealing with a nation still alive, still contributing its strength to spin the wheel of the world around, then are his labours worthless and his brains misused. I would tell him that if his work is paid for, then is he a robber if he gives no return in information which will be of practical service to Egypt in some way or another. The Egyptian Government spends enormous sums each year upon the preservation of the magnificent relics of bygone ages—relics for which, I regret to say, the Egyptians themselves care extremely little. Is this money spent, then, to amuse the tourist in the land, or simply to fulfil obligations to ethical susceptibilities? No; there is but one justification for this very necessary expenditure of public money—namely, that these relics are regarded, so to speak, as the school-books of the nation, which range over a series of subjects from pottery-making to politics, from stone-cutting to statecraft. The future of Egypt may be read upon the walls of her ancient temples and tombs. Let the Egyptologist never forget, in the interest and excitement of his discoveries, what is the real object of his work.

# CHAPTER III.

## THE NECESSITY OF ARCHÆOLOGY TO THE GAIETY OF THE WORLD.

When a great man puts a period to his existence upon earth by dying, he is carefully buried in a tomb, and a monument is set up to his glory in the neighbouring church. He may then be said to begin his second life, his life in the memory of the chronicler and historian. After the lapse of an æon or two the works of the historian, and perchance the tomb itself, are rediscovered; and the great man begins his third life, now as a subject of discussion and controversy amongst archæologists in the pages of a scientific journal. It may be supposed that the spirit of the great man, not a little pleased with its second life, has an extreme distaste for his third. There is a dead atmosphere about it which sets him yawning as only his grave yawned before. The charm has been taken from his deeds; there is no longer any spring in them. He must feel towards the archæologist much as a young man feels towards his cold-blooded parent by whom his love affair has just been found out. The public, too, if by chance it comes upon this archæological journal, finds the discussion nothing more than a mental gymnastic, which, as the reader drops off to sleep, gives him the impression that the writer is a man of profound brain capacity, but, like the remains of the great man of olden times, as dry as dust.

There is one thing, however, which has been overlooked. This scientific journal does not contain the ultimate results of the archæologist's researches. It contains the researches themselves. The public, so to speak, has been listening to the pianist playing his morning scales, has been watching the artist mixing his colours, has been examining the unshaped block of marble and the chisels in the sculptor's studio. It must be confessed, of course, that the archæologist has so enjoyed his researches that often the ultimate result has been overlooked by him. In the case of Egyptian archæology, for example, there are only two Egyptologists who have ever set themselves to write a readable history,[1] whereas the number of books which record the facts of the science is legion.

The archæologist not infrequently lives, for a large part of his time, in a museum, a somewhat dismal place. He is surrounded by rotting tapestries, decaying bones, crumbling stones, and rusted or corroded objects. His indoor work has paled his cheek, and his muscles are not like iron bands. He stands, often, in the contiguity to an ancient broadsword most fitted to demonstrate the fact that he could never use it. He would probably be dismissed his curatorship were he to tell of any dreams which might run in his head—dreams of the time when those tapestries hung upon the walls of barons' banquet-halls, or when those stones rose high above the streets of Camelot.

Moreover, those who make researches independently must needs contribute their results to scientific journals, written in the jargon of the learned. I came across a now forgotten journal, a short time ago, in which an English gentleman, believing that he had made a discovery in the province of Egyptian hieroglyphs, announced it in ancient Greek. There would be no supply of such pedantic swagger were there not a demand for it.

Small wonder, then, that the archæologist is often represented as partaking somewhat of the quality of the dust amidst which he works. It is not necessary here to discuss whether this estimate is just or not: I wish only to point out its paradoxical nature.

More than any other science, archæology might be expected to supply its exponents with stuff that, like old wine, would fire the blood

1 Professor J.H. Breasted and Sir Gaston Maspero.

and stimulate the senses. The stirring events of the Past must often be reconstructed by the archæologist with such precision that his prejudices are aroused, and his sympathies are so enlisted as to set him fighting with a will under this banner or under that. The noise of the hardy strife of young nations is not yet silenced for him, nor have the flags and the pennants faded from sight. He has knowledge of the state secrets of kings, and, all along the line, is an intimate spectator of the crowded pageant of history. The caravan-masters of the elder days, the admirals of the "great green sea" the captains of archers, have related their adventures to him; and he might repeat to you their stories. Indeed, he has such a tale to tell that, looking at it in this light, one might expect his listeners all to be good fighting men and noble women. It might be supposed that the archæologist would gather around him only men who have pleasure in the road that leads over the hills, and women who have known the delight of the open. One has heard so often of the "brave days of old" that the archæologist might well be expected to have his head stuffed with brave tales and little else.

His range, however, may be wider than this. To him, perhaps, it has been given to listen to the voice of the ancient poet, heard as a far-off whisper; to breathe in forgotten gardens the perfume of long dead flowers; to contemplate the love of women whose beauty is all perished in the dust; to hearken to the sound of the harp and the sistra, to be the possessor of the riches of historical romance. Dim armies have battled around him for the love of Helen; shadowy captains of sea-going ships have sung to him through the storm the song of the sweethearts left behind them; he has feasted with sultans, and kings' goblets have been held to his lips; he has watched Uriah the Hittite sent to the forefront of the battle.

Thus, were he to offer a story, one might now suppose that there would gather around him, not the men of muscle, but a throng of sallow listeners, as improperly expectant as were those who hearkened under the moon to the narrations of Boccaccio, or, in old Baghdad, gave ear to the tales of the thousand and one nights. One might suppose that his audience would be drawn from those classes most fondly addicted to pleasure, or most nearly representative, in their land and in their time, of the light-hearted and not unwanton races of whom he had to tell. For his story might be expected to be one wherein wine and women and song found countenance. Even were he to tell of ancient tragedies and old sorrows, he would still make his appeal, one might suppose, to gallants and their mistresses, to sporting men and women of fashion, just as, in the mournful song of Rosabelle, Sir Walter Scott is able to address himself to the "ladies gay," or Coleridge in his sad "Ballad of the Dark Ladie" to "fair maids."

Who could better arrest the attention of the coxcomb than the archæologist who has knowledge of silks and scents now lost to the living world? To the gourmet who could more appeal than the archæologist who has made abundant acquaintance with the forgotten dishes of the East? Who could so surely thrill the senses of the courtesan than the archæologist who can relate that which was whispered by Anthony in the ear of Cleopatra? To the gambler who could be more enticing than the archæologist who has seen kings play at dice for their kingdoms? The imaginative, truly, might well collect the most highly disreputable audience to listen to the tales of the archæologist.

But no, these are not the people who are anxious to catch the pearls which drop from his mouth. Do statesmen and diplomatists, then, listen to him who can unravel for them the policies of the Past? Do business men hasten from Threadneedle Street and Wall Street to sit at his feet, that they may have instilled into them a little of the romance of ancient money? I fear not.

Come with me to some provincial town, where this day Professor Blank is to deliver one of his archæological lectures at the Town Hall. We are met at the door by the secretary of the local archæological society: a melancholy lady in green plush, who suffers from St Vitus's dance. Gloomily we enter the hall and silently accept the seats which are indicated to us by an unfortunate gentleman with a club-foot. In front of us an elderly female with short hair is chatting to a very plain young woman draped like a lay figure. On the right an emaciated man with a very bad cough shuffles on his chair; on the left two old grey-beards grumble to one another about the weather, a subject which leads up to the familiar "Mine catches me in the small of the back"; while behind us the inevitable curate, of whose appearance it would be trite to speak, describes to an astonished old lady the recent discovery of the pelvis of a mastodon.

The professor and the aged chairman step on to the platform; and, amidst the profoundest gloom, the latter rises to pronounce the prefatory rigmarole. "Archæology," he says, in a voice of brass, "is a science which bars its doors to all but the most erudite; for, to the layman who has not been vouchsafed the opportunity of studying the dusty volumes of the learned, the bones of the dead will not reveal their secrets, nor will the crumbling pediments of naos and cenotaph, the obliterated tombstones, or the worm-eaten parchments, tell us their story. Tonight, however, we are privileged; for Professor Blank will open the doors for us that we may gaze for a moment upon that solemn charnel-house of the Past in which he has sat for so many long hours of inductive meditation."

And the professor by his side, whose head, perhaps, was filled with the martial music of the long-lost hosts of the Lord, or before whose eyes there swayed the entrancing forms of the dancing-girls of Babylon, stares horrified from chairman to audience. He sees crabbed old men and barren old women before him, afflicted youths and fatuous maidens; and he realises at once that the golden keys which he possesses to the gates of the treasury of the jewelled Past will not open the doors of that charnel-house which they desire to be shown. The scent of the king's roses fades from his nostrils, the Egyptian music which throbbed in his ears is hushed, the glorious illumination of the Palace of a Thousand Columns is extinguished; and in the gathering gloom we leave him fumbling with a rusty key at the mildewed door of the Place of Bones.

Why is it, one asks, that archæology is a thing so misunderstood? Can it be that both lecturer and audience have crushed down that which was in reality uppermost in their minds: that a shy search for romance has led these people to the Town Hall? Or perchance archæology has become to them something not unlike a vice, and to listen to an archæological lecture is their remaining chance of being naughty. It may be that, having one foot in the grave, they take pleasure in kicking the moss from the surrounding tombstones with the other; or that, being denied, for one reason or another, the jovial society of the living, like Robert Southey's "Scholar" their hopes are with the dead.

PL. VI. A relief upon the side of the sarcophagus of one of the wives of King Mentuhotep III., discovered at Dêr el Bahri (Thebes). The royal lady is taking sweet-smelling ointment from an alabaster vase. A handmaiden keeps the flies away with a bird's-wing fan.—CAIRO MUSEUM.]
*[Photo by E. Brugsch Pasha.*

Be the explanation what it may, the fact is indisputable that archæology is patronised by those who know not its real meaning. A man has no more right to think of the people of old as dust and dead bones than he has to think of his contemporaries as lumps of meat. The true archæologist does not take pleasure in skeletons as skeletons, for his whole effort is to cover them decently with flesh and skin once more, and to put some thoughts back into the empty skulls. He sets himself to hide again the things which he would not intentionally lay bare. Nor does he delight in ruined buildings: rather he deplores that they are ruined. Coleridge wrote like the true archæologist when he composed that most magical poem "Khubla Khan"—

"In Xanadu did Khubla Khan
A stately pleasure-dome decree:
Where Alph, the sacred river, ran
Through caverns measureless to man
Down to a sunless sea."

And those who would have the pleasure-domes of the gorgeous Past reconstructed for them must turn to the archæologist; those who would see the damsel with the dulcimer in the gardens of Xanadu must ask of him the secret, and of none other. It is true that, before he can refashion the dome or the damsel, he will have to grub his way through old refuse heaps till he shall lay bare the ruins of the walls and expose the bones of the lady. But this is the "dirty work"; and the mistake which is made lies here: that this preliminary dirty work is confused with the final clean result. An artist will sometimes build up his picture of Venus from a skeleton bought from an old Jew round the corner; and the smooth white paper which he uses will have been made from putrid rags and bones. Amongst painters themselves these facts are not hidden, but by the public they are most carefully obscured. In the case of archæology, however, the tedious details of construction are so placed in the foreground that the final picture is hardly noticed at all. As well might one go to Rheims to see men fly, and be shown nothing else but screws and nuts, steel rods and cog-wheels. Originally the fault, perhaps, lay with the archæologist; now it lies both with him and with the public. The public has learnt to ask to be shown the works, and the archæologist is often so proud of them that he forgets to mention the purpose of the machine.

A Roman statue of bronze, let us suppose, is discovered in the Thames valley. It is so corroded and eaten away that only an expert could recognise that it represents a reclining goddess. In this condition it is placed in the museum, and a photograph of it is published in 'The Graphic.' Those who come to look at it in its glass case think it is a bunch of grapes, or possibly a monkey: those who see its photograph say that it is more probably an irregular catapult-stone or a fish in convulsions.

The archæologist alone holds its secret, and only he can see it as it was. He alone can know the mind of the artist who made it, or interpret the full meaning of the conception. It might have been expected, then, that the public would demand, and the archæologist delightedly furnish, a model of the figure as near to the original as possible; or, failing that, a restoration in drawing, or even a worded description of its original beauty. But no: the public, if it wants anything, wants to see the shapeless object in all its corrosion; and the archæologist forgets that it is blind to aught else but that corrosion. One of the main duties of the archæologist is thus lost sight of: his duty as Interpreter and Remembrancer of the Past.

All the riches of olden times, all the majesty, all the power, are the inheritance of the present day; and the archæologist is the recorder of this fortune. He must deal in dead bones only so far as the keeper of a financial fortune must deal in dry documents. Behind those documents glitters the gold, and behind those bones shines the wonder of the things that were. And when an object once beautiful has by age become unsightly, one might suppose that he would wish to show it to none save his colleagues or the reasonably curious layman. When a man makes the statement that his grandmother, now in her ninety-ninth year, was once a beautiful woman, he does not go and find her to prove his words and bring her tottering into the room: he shows a picture of her as she was; or, if he cannot find one, he describes what good evidence tells him was her probable appearance. In allowing his controlled and sober imagination thus to perform its natural functions, though it would never do to tell his grandmother so, he becomes an archæologist, a remembrancer of the Past.

In the case of archæology, however, the public does not permit itself so to be convinced. In the Ashmolean Museum at Oxford excellent facsimile electrotypes of early Greek weapons are exhibited; and these have far more value in bringing the Past before us than the actual weapons of that period, corroded and broken, would have. But the visitor says, "These are shams," and passes on.

It will be seen, then, that the business of archæology is often misunderstood both by archæologists and by the public; and that there is really no reason to believe, with Thomas Earle, that the real antiquarian loves a thing the better for that it is rotten and stinketh. That the impression has gone about is his own fault, for he has exposed too much to view the mechanism of his work; but it is also the fault of the public for not asking of him a picture of things as they were.

Man is by nature a creature of the present. It is only by an effort that he can consider the future, it is often quite impossible for him to give any heed at all to the Past. The days of old are so blurred and remote that it seems right to him that any relic from them should, by the maltreatment of Time, be unrecognisable. The finding of an old sword, half-eaten by rust, will only please him in so far as it shows him once more by its sad condition the great gap between those days and these, and convinces him again of the sole importance of the present. The archæologist, he will tell you, is a fool if he expects him to be interested in a wretched old bit of scrap-iron. He is right. It would be as rash to suppose that he would find interest in an ancient sword in its rusted condition as it would be to expect the spectator at Rheims to find fascination in the nuts and screws. The true archæologist would hide that corroded weapon in his workshop, where his fellow-workers alone could see it. For he recognises that it is only the sword which is as good as new that impresses the public; it is only the Present that counts. That is the real reason why he is an archæologist. He has turned to the Past because he is in love with the Present. He, more than any man, worships at the altar of the goddess of Today; and he is so desirous of extending her dominion that he has adventured, like a crusader, into the lands of the Past in order to subject them to her. Adoring the Now, he would resent the publicity of anything which so obviously suggested the Then as a rust-eaten old blade. His whole business is to hide the gap between Yesterday and Today; and, unless a man is initiate, he would have him either see the perfect sword as it was when it sought the foeman's bowels, or see nothing. The Present is too small for him; and it is therefore that he calls so insistently to the Past to come forth from the darkness to augment it. The ordinary man lives in the Present, and he will tell one that the archæologist lives in the Past. This is not so. The layman, in the manner of the Little Englander, lives in a small and confined Present; but the archæologist, like a true Imperialist, ranges through all time, and calls it not the Past but the Greater Present.

The archæologist is not, or ought not to be, lacking in vivacity. One might say that he is so sensible to the charms of society that, finding his companions too few in number, he has drawn the olden times to him to search them for jovial men and agreeable women. It might be added that he has so laughed at jest and joke that, fearing lest the funds of humour run dry, he has gathered the laughter of all the years to his enrichment. Certainly he has so delighted in noble adventure and stirring action that he finds his newspaper insufficient to his needs, and fetches to his aid the tales of old heroes. In fact, the archæologist is so enamoured of life that he would raise all the dead from their graves. He will not have it that the men of old are dust: he would bring them to him to share with him the sunlight which he finds so precious. He is so much an enemy of Death and Decay that he would rob them of their harvest; and, for every life the foe has claimed, he would raise up, if he could, a memory that would continue to live.

The meaning of the heading which has been given to this chapter is now becoming clear, and the direction of the argument is already apparent. So far it has been my purpose to show that the archæologist is not a rag-and-bone man, though the public generally thinks he is, and he often thinks he is himself. The attempt has been made to suggest that archæology ought not to consist in sitting in a charnel-house amongst the dead, but rather in ignoring that place and taking the bones into the light of day, decently clad in flesh and finery. It has now to be shown in what manner this parading of the Past is needful to the gaiety of the Present.

Amongst cultured people whose social position makes it difficult for them to dance in circles on the grass in order to express or to stimulate their gaiety, and whose school of deportment will not permit them to sing a merry song of sixpence as they trip down the streets, there is some danger of the fire of merriment dying for want of fuel. Vivacity in printed books, therefore, has been encouraged, so that the mind at least, if not the body, may skip about and clap its hands. A portly gentleman with a solemn face, reading his 'Punch' in the club, is, after all, giving play to precisely those same humours which in ancient days might have led him, like Georgy Porgy, to kiss the girls or to perform any other merry joke. It is necessary, therefore, ever to enlarge the stock of things humorous, vivacious, or rousing, if thoughts are to be kept young and eyes bright in this age of restraint. What would Yuletide be without the olden times to bolster it? What would the Christmas numbers do without the pictures of our great-grandparents' coaches snow-bound, of huntsmen of the eighteenth century, of jesters at the courts of the barons? What should we do without the 'Vicar of Wakefield,' the 'Compleat Angler,' 'Pepys' Diary,' and all the rest of the ancient books? And, going back a few centuries, what an amount we should miss had we not 'Æsop's Fables,' the 'Odyssey,' the tales of the Trojan War, and so on. It is from the archæologist that one must expect the augmentation of this supply; and just in that degree in which the existing supply is really a necessary part of our equipment, so archæology, which looks for more, is necessary to our gaiety.

PL. VII. Lady rouging herself: she holds a mirror and rouge-pot.—FROM A PAPYRUS, TURIN.

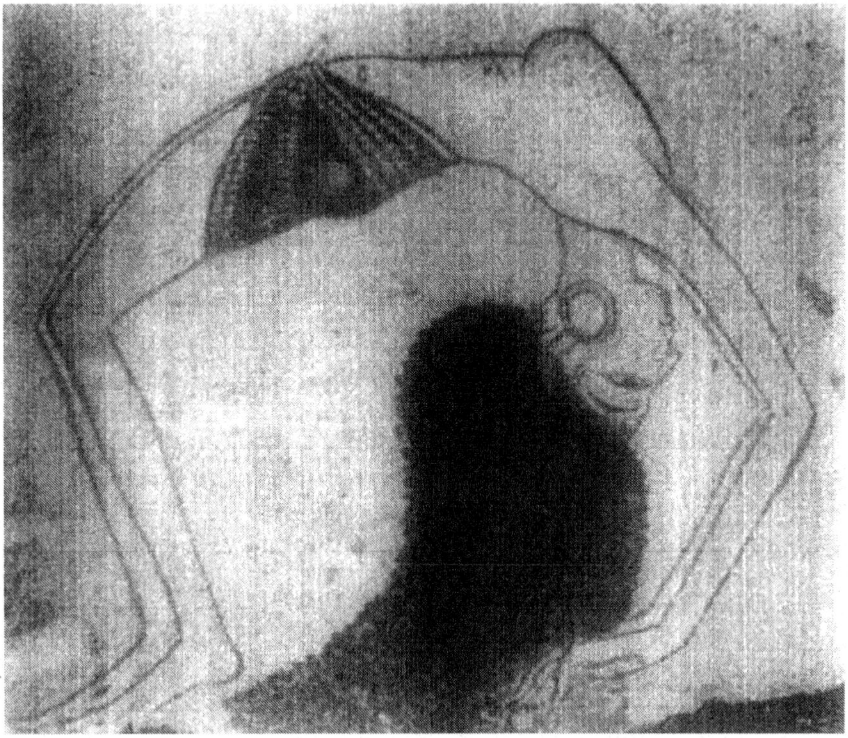

Dancing girl turning a back somersault.
—NEW KINGDOM.

In order to keep his intellect undulled by the routine of his dreary work, Matthew Arnold was wont to write a few lines of poetry each day. Poetry, like music and song, is an effective dispeller of care; and those who find Omar Khayyam or "In Memoriam" incapable of removing the of burden of their woes, will no doubt appreciate the "Owl and the Pussy-cat," or the Bab Ballads. In some form or other verse and song are closely linked with happiness; and a ditty from any age has its interests and its charm.

"She gazes at the stars above:
    I would I were the skies,
That I might gaze upon my love
    With such a thousand eyes!"

That is probably from the Greek of Plato, a writer who is not much read by the public at large, and whose works are the legitimate property of the antiquarian. It suffices to show that it is not only to the moderns that we have to look for dainty verse that is conducive to a light heart. The following lines are from the ancient Egyptian:—

"While in my room I lie all day
In pain that will not pass away,
    The neighbours come and go.
Ah, if with them my darling came
The doctors would be put to shame:
    *She* understands my woe."

Such examples might be multiplied indefinitely; and the reader will admit that there is as much of a lilt about those which are here quoted as there is about the majority of the ditties which he has hummed to himself in his hour of contentment. Here is Philodemus' description of his mistress's charms:—

"My lady-love is small and brown;
My lady's skin is soft as down;
Her hair like parseley twists and turns;
Her voice with magic passion burns . . ."

And here is an ancient Egyptian's description of not very dissimilar phenomena:—

"A damsel sweet unto the sight,
    A maid of whom no like there is;
Black are her tresses as the night,
    And blacker than the blackberries."

Does not the archæologist perform a service to his contemporaries by searching out such rhymes and delving for more? They bring with them, moreover, so subtle a suggestion of bygone romance, they are backed by so fair a scene of Athenian luxury or Theban splendour, that they possess a charm not often felt in modern verse. If it is argued that there is no need to increase the present supply of such ditties, since they are really quite unessential to our gaiety, the answer may be given that no nation and no period has ever found them unessential; and a light heart has been expressed in this manner since man came down from the trees.

Let us turn now to another consideration. For a man to be light of heart he must have confidence in humanity. He cannot greet the morn with a smiling countenance if he believes that he and his fellows are slipping down the broad path which leads to destruction. The archæologist never despairs of mankind; for he has seen nations rise and fall till he is almost giddy, but he knows that there has never been a general deterioration. He realises that though a great nation may suffer defeat and annihilation, it is possible for it to go down in such a thunder that the talk of it stimulates other nations for all time. He sees, if any man can, that all things work together for happiness. He has observed the cycle of events, the good years and the bad; and in an evil time he is comforted by the knowledge that the good will presently roll round again. Thus the lesson which he can teach is a very real necessity to that contentment of mind which lies at the root of all gaiety.

Again, a man cannot be permanently happy unless he has a just sense of proportion. He who is too big for his boots must needs limp; and he who has a swollen head is in perpetual discomfort. The history of the lives of men, the history of the nations, gives one a fairer sense of proportion than does almost any other study. In the great company of the men of old he cannot fail to assess his true value: if he has any conceit there is a greater than he to snub him; if he has a poor opinion of his powers there is many a fool with whom to contrast himself favourably. If he would risk his fortune on the spinning of a coin, being aware of the prevalence of his good-luck, archæology will tell him that the best luck will change; or if, when in sore straits, he asks whether ever a man was so unlucky, archæology will answer him that many millions of men have been more unfavoured than he. Archæology provides a precedent for almost every event or occurrence where modern inventions are not involved; and, in this manner, one may reckon their value and determine their trend. Thus many of the small worries which cause so leaden a weight to lie upon the heart and mind are by the archæologist ignored; and many of the larger calamities by him are met with serenity.

But not only does the archæologist learn to estimate himself and his actions: he learns also to see the relationship in which his life stands to the course of Time. Without archæology a man may be disturbed lest the world be about to come to an end: after a study of history he knows that it has only just begun; and that gaiety which is said to have obtained "when the world was young" is to him, therefore, a present condition. By studying the ages the archæologist learns to reckon in units of a thousand years; and it is only then that that little unit of threescore-and-ten falls into its proper proportion. "A thousand ages in Thy sight are like an evening gone," says the hymn, but it is only the archæologist who knows the meaning of the words; and it is only he who can explain that great discrepancy in the Christian faith between the statement "Behold, I come quickly" and the actual fact. A man who knows where he is in regard to his fellows, and realises where he stands in regard to Time, has learnt a lesson of archæology which is as necessary to his peace of mind as his peace of mind is necessary to his gaiety.

It is not needful, however, to continue to point out the many ways in which archæology may be shown to be necessary to happiness. The reader will have comprehended the trend of the argument, and, if he be in sympathy with it, he will not be unwilling to develop the theme for himself. Only one point, therefore, need here be taken up. It has been reserved to the end of this chapter, for, by its nature, it closes all arguments. I refer to Death.

Death, as we watch it around us, is the black menace of the heavens which darkens every man's day; Death, coming to our neighbour, puts a period to our merry-making; Death, seen close beside us, calls a halt in our march of pleasure. But let those who would wrest her victory from the grave turn to a study of the Past, where all is dead yet still lives, and they will find that the horror of life's cessation is materially lessened. To those who are familiar with the course of history, Death seems, to some extent, but the happy solution of the dilemma of life. So many men have welcomed its coming that one begins to feel that it cannot be so very terrible. Of the death of a certain Pharaoh an ancient Egyptian wrote: "He goes to heaven like the hawks, and his feathers are like those of the geese; he rushes at heaven like a crane, he kisses heaven like the falcon, he leaps to heaven like the locust"; and we who read these words can feel that to rush eagerly at heaven like the crane would be a mighty fine ending of the pother. Archæology, and especially Egyptology, in this respect is a bulwark to those who find the faith of their fathers wavering; for, after much study, the triumphant assertion which is so often found in Egyptian tombs—"Thou dost not come dead to thy sepulchre, thou comest living"—begins to take hold of the imagination. Death has been the parent of so much goodness, dying men have cut such a dash, that one looks at it with an awakening interest. Even if the sense of the misfortune of death is uppermost in an archæologist's mind, he may find not a little comfort in having before him the example of so many good, men, who, in their hour, have faced that great calamity with squared shoulders.

"When Death comes," says a certain sage of ancient Egypt, "it seizes the babe that is on the breast of its mother as well as he that has become an old man. When thy messenger comes to carry thee away, be thou found by him *ready*." Why, here is our chance; here is the opportunity for that flourish which modesty, throughout our life, has forbidden to us! John Tiptoft, Earl of Worcester, when the time came for him to lay his head upon the block, bade the executioner smite it off with three strokes as a courtesy to the Holy Trinity. King Charles the Second, as he lay upon his death-bed, apologised to those who stood around him for "being an unconscionable time adying." The story is familiar of Napoleon's aide-de-camp, who, when he had been asked whether he were wounded, replied, "Not wounded: killed," and thereupon expired. The Past is full of such incidents; and so inspiring are they that Death comes to be regarded as a most stirring adventure. The archæologist, too, better than any other, knows the vastness of the dead men's majority; and if, like the ancients, he believes in the Elysian fields, where no death is and decay is unknown, he alone will realise the excellent nature of the company into which he will there be introduced.

There is, however, far more living going on in the world than dying; and there is more happiness (thanks be!) than sorrow. Thus the archæologist has a great deal more of pleasure than of pain to give to us for our enrichment. The reader will here enter an objection. He will say: "This may be true of archæology in general, but in the case of Egyptology, with which we are here mostly concerned, he surely has to deal with a sad and solemn people." The answer will be found in the next chapter. No nation in the world's history has been so gay, so light-hearted as the ancient Egyptians; and Egyptology furnishes, perhaps, the most convincing proof that archæology is, or should be, a merry science, very necessary to the gaiety of the world. I defy a man suffering from his liver to understand the old Egyptians; I defy a man who does not appreciate the pleasure of life to make anything of them. Egyptian archæology presents a pageant of such brilliancy that the archæologist is often carried along by it as in a dream, down the valley and over the hills, till, Past blending with Present, and Present with Future, he finds himself led to a kind of Island of the Blest, where death is forgotten and only the joy of life, and life's good deeds, still remain; where pleasure-domes, and all the ancient "miracles of rare device," rise into the air from above the flowers; and where the damsel with the dulcimer beside the running stream sings to him of Mount Abora and of the old heroes of the elder days. If the Egyptologist or the archæologist could revive within him one-hundredth part of the elusive romance, the delicate gaiety, the subtle humour, the intangible tenderness, the unspeakable goodness, of much that is to be found in his province, one would have to cry, like Coleridge—

"Beware, beware!
Weave a circle round him thrice,
And close your eyes with holy dread,
For he on honey-dew hath fed,
And drunk the milk of Paradise."

# PART II.

# STUDIES IN THE TREASURY.

"And I could tell thee stories that would make thee laugh at all thy trouble, and take thee to a land of which thou hast never even dreamed. Where the trees have ever blossoms, and are noisy with the humming of intoxicated bees. Where by day the suns are never burning, and by night the moonstones ooze with nectar in the rays of the camphor-laden moon. Where the blue lakes are filled with rows of silver swans, and where, on steps of lapis lazuli, the peacocks dance in agitation at the murmur of the thunder in the hills. Where the lightning flashes without harming, to light the way to women stealing in the darkness to meetings with their lovers, and the rainbow hangs for ever like an opal on the dark blue curtain of the cloud. Where, on the moonlit roofs of crystal palaces, pairs of lovers laugh at the reflection of each other's love-sick faces in goblets of red wine, breathing, as they drink, air heavy with the fragrance of the sandal, wafted on the breezes from the mountain of the south. Where they play and pelt each other with emeralds and rubies, fetched at the churning of the ocean from the bottom of the sea. Where rivers, whose sands are always golden, flow slowly past long lines of silent cranes that hunt for silver fishes in the rushes on the banks. Where men are true, and maidens love for ever, and the lotus never fades."

F.W. BAIN: *A Heifer of the Dawn.*

# CHAPTER IV.

## THE TEMPERAMENT OF THE ANCIENT EGYPTIANS.

A certain school geography book, now out of date, condenses its remarks upon the character of our Gallic cousins into the following pregnant sentence: "The French are a gay and frivolous nation, fond of dancing and red wine." The description would so nearly apply to the ancient inhabitants of Egypt, that its adoption here as a text to this chapter cannot be said to be extravagant. The unbiassed inquirer into the affairs of ancient Egypt must discover ultimately, and perhaps to his regret, that the dwellers on the Nile were a "gay and frivolous people," festive, light-hearted, and mirthful, "fond of dancing and red wine," and pledged to all that is brilliant in life. There are very many people, naturally, who hold to those views which their forefathers held before them, and picture the Egyptians as a sombre, gloomy people; replete with thoughts of Death and of the more melancholy aspect of religion; burdened with the menacing presence of a multitude of horrible gods and demons, whose priests demanded the erection of vast temples for their appeasement; having little joy of this life, and much uneasy conjecture about the next; making entertainment in solemn gatherings and ponderous feasts; and holding merriment in holy contempt. Of the five startling classes into which the dictionary divides the human temperament, namely, the bilious or choleric, the phlegmatic, the sanguine, the melancholic, and the nervous, it is probable that the first, the second, and the fourth would be those assigned to the ancient Egyptians by these people. This view is so entirely false that one will be forgiven if, in the attempt to dissolve it, the gaiety of the race is thrust before the reader with too little extenuation. The sanguine, and perhaps the nervous, are the classes of temperament under which the Egyptians must be docketed. It cannot be denied that they were an industrious and even a strenuous people, that they indulged in the most serious thoughts, and attempted to study the most complex problems of life, and that the ceremonial side of their religion occupied a large part of their time. But there is abundant evidence to show that, like their descendents of the present day, they were one of the least gloomy people of the world, and that they took their duties in the most buoyant manner, allowing as much sunshine to radiate through their minds as shone from the cloudless Egyptian skies upon their dazzling country.

PL. VIII. Two Egyptian boys decked with flowers and a third holding a musical instrument. They are standing against the outside wall of theDendereh Temple.

*[Photo by E. Bird.]*

It is curiously interesting to notice how general is the present belief in the solemnity of this ancient race's attitude towards existence, and how little their real character is appreciated. Already the reader will be protesting, perhaps, that the application of the geographer's summary of French characteristics to the ancient Egyptians lessens in no wise its ridiculousness, but rather increases it. Let the protest, however, be held back for a while. Even if the Egyptians were not always frivolous, they were always uncommonly gay, and any slight exaggeration will be pardoned in view of the fact that old prejudices have to be violently overturned, and the stigma of melancholy and ponderous sobriety torn from the national name. It would be a matter of little surprise to some good persons if the products of excavation in the Nile Valley consisted largely of antique black kid gloves.

Like many other nations the ancient Egyptians rendered mortuary service to their ancestors, and solid tomb-chapels had to be constructed in honour of the more important dead. Both for the purpose of preserving the mummy intact, and also in order to keep the ceremonies going for as long a period of time as possible, these chapels were constructed in a most substantial manner, and many of them have withstood successfully the siege of the years. The dwelling-houses, on the other hand, were seldom delivered from father to son; but, as in modern Egypt, each grandee built a palace for himself, designed to last for a lifetime only, and hardly one of these mansions still exists even as a ruin.

Moreover the tombs were constructed in the dry desert or in the solid hillside, whereas the dwelling-houses were situated on the damp earth, where they had little chance of remaining undemolished. And so it is that the main part of our knowledge of the Egyptians is derived from a study of their tombs and mortuary temples. How false would be our estimate of the character of a modern nation were we to glean our information solely from its churchyard inscriptions! We should know absolutely nothing of the frivolous side of the life of those whose bare bones lie beneath the gloomy declaration of their Christian virtues. It will be realised how sincere was the light-heartedness of the Egyptians when it is remembered that almost everything in the following record of their gaieties is derived from a study of the tombs, and of objects found therein.

Light-heartedness is the key-note of the ancient philosophy of the country, and in this assertion the reader will, in most cases, find cause for surprise. The Greek travellers in Egypt, who returned to their native land impressed with the wonderful mysticism of the Egyptians, committed their amazement to paper, and so led off that feeling of awed reverence which is felt for the philosophy of Pharaoh's subjects. But in their case there was the presence of the priests and wise men eloquently to baffle them into the state of respect, and there were a thousand unwritten arguments, comments, articles of faith, and controverted points of doctrine heard from the mouths of the believers, to surprise them into a reverential attitude. But we of the present day have left to us only the more outward and visible remains of the Egyptians. There are only the fundamental doctrines to work on, the more penetrating notes of the harmony to listen to. Thus the outline of the philosophy is able to be studied without any complication, and we have no whirligig of priestly talk to confuse it. Examined in this way, working only from cold stones and dry papyri, we are confronted with the old "Eat, drink, and be merry," which is at once the happiest and most dangerous philosophy conceived by man. It is to be noticed that this way of looking at life is to be found in Egypt from the earliest times down to the period of the Greek occupation of the country, and, in fact, until the present day. That is to say, it was a philosophy inborn in the Egyptian,—a part of his nature.

Imhotep, the famous philosopher of Dynasty III., about B.C. 3000, said to his disciples: "Behold the dwellings of the dead. Their walls fall down, their place is no more; they are as though they had never existed"; and he drew from this the lesson that man is soon done with and forgotten, and that therefore his life should be as happy as possible. To Imhotep must be attributed the earliest known exhortation to man to resign himself to his candle-end of a life, and to the inevitable snuffing-out to come, and to be merry while yet he may. There is a poem, dating from about B.C. 2000, from which the following is taken:—

> "Walk after thy heart's desire so long as thou livest. Put myrrh on thy head, clothe thyself in fine linen, anoint thyself with the true marvels of God . . . Let not thy heart concern itself, until there cometh to thee that great day of lamentation. Yet he who is at rest can hear not thy complaint, and he who lies in the tomb can understand not thy weeping. Therefore, with smiling face, let thy days be happy, and rest not therein. For no man carrieth his goods away with him; "O, no man returneth again who is gone thither."

Again, we have the same sentiments expressed in a tomb of about B.C. 1350, belonging to a certain Neferhotep, a priest of Amen. It is quoted on page 235, and here we need only note the ending:

> "Come, songs and music are before thee. Set behind thee all cares; think only upon gladness, until that day cometh whereon thou shalt go down to the land which loveth silence."

A Ptolemaic inscription quoted more fully towards the end of this chapter reads: "Follow thy desire by night and by day. Put not care within thy heart."

The ancient Egyptian peasants, like their modern descendants, were fatalists, and a happy carelessness seems to have softened the strenuousness of their daily tasks. The peasants of the present day in Egypt so lack the initiative to develop the scope of their industries that their life cannot be said to be strenuous. In whatever work they undertake, however, they show a wonderful degree of cheerfulness, and a fine disregard for misfortune. Their forefathers, similarly, went through their labours with a song upon their lips. In the tombs at Sakkâra, dating from the Old

Empire, there are scenes representing flocks of goats treading in the seed on the newly-sown ground, and the inscriptions give the song which the goat-herds sing:—

"The goat-herd is in the water with the fishes,—
He speaks with the *nar*-fish, he talks with the pike;
From the west is your goat-herd; your goat-herd is from the west."

The meaning of the words is not known, of course, but the song seems to have been a popular one. A more comprehensible ditty is that sung to the oxen by their driver, which dates from the New Empire:—

"Thresh out for yourselves, ye oxen, thresh out for yourselves.
Thresh out the straw for your food, and the grain for your masters.
Do not rest yourselves, for it is cool today."

Some of the love-songs have been preserved from destruction, and these throw much light upon the subject of the Egyptian temperament. A number of songs, supposed to have been sung by a girl to her lover, form themselves into a collection entitled "The beautiful and gladsome songs of thy sister, whom thy heart loves, as she walks in the fields." The girl is supposed to belong to the peasant class, and most of the verses are sung whilst she is at her daily occupation of snaring wild duck in the marshes. One must imagine the songs warbled without any particular refrain, just as in the case of the modern Egyptians, who pour out their ancient tales of love and adventure in a series of bird-like cadences, full-throated, and often wonderfully melodious. A peculiar sweetness and tenderness will be noticed in the following examples, and though they suffer in translation, their airy lightness and refinement is to be distinguished. One characteristic song, addressed by the girl to her lover, runs—

"Caught by the worm, the wild duck cries,
But in the love-light of thine eyes
I, trembling, loose the trap. So flies
The bird into the air.
What will my angry mother say?
With basket full I come each day,
But now thy love hath led me stray,
And I have set no snare."

Again, in a somewhat similar strain, she sings—

"The wild duck scatter far, and now
Again they light upon the bough
And cry unto their kind;
Anon they gather on the mere—
But yet unharmed I leave them there,
For love hath filled my mind."

Another song must be given here in prose form. The girl who sings it is supposed to be making a wreath of flowers, and as she works she cries—

> "I am thy first sister, and to me thou art as a garden which I have planted with flowers and all sweet-smelling herbs. And I have directed a canal into it, that thou mightest dip thy hand into it when the north wind blows cool. The place is beautiful where we walk, because we walk together, thy hand resting within mine, our mind thoughtful and our heart joyful. It is intoxicating to me to hear thy voice, yet my life depends upon hearing it. Whenever I see thee it is better to me than food and drink."

One more song must be quoted, for it is so artless and so full of human tenderness that I may risk the accusation of straying from the main argument in repeating it. It runs:—

"The breath of thy nostrils alone
Is that which maketh my heart to live.
I found thee:
God grant thee to me
For ever and ever."

It is really painful to think of these words as having fallen from the lips of what is now a resin-smelling lump of bones and hardened flesh, perhaps still unearthed, perhaps lying in some museum show-case, or perhaps kicked about in fragments over the hot sand of some tourist-crowded necropolis. Mummies are the most lifeless objects one could well imagine. It is impossible even for those whose imaginations are most powerful, to infuse life into a thing so utterly dead as an embalmed body; and this fact is partly responsible for that atmosphere of stark, melancholy, sobriety and aloofness which surrounds the affairs of ancient Egypt. In reading these verses, it is imperative for their right understanding that the mummies and their resting-places should be banished from the thoughts. It is not always a simple matter for the student to rid himself of the atmosphere of the museum, where the beads which should be jangling on a brown neck are lying numbered and labelled on red velvet; where the bird-trap, once the centre of such feathered commotion, is propped up in a glass case as "D, 18,432"; and where even the document in which the verses are written is the lawful booty of the grammarian and philologist in the library. But it is the first duty of an archæologist to do away with that atmosphere.

Let those who are untrammelled then, pass out into the sunshine of the Egyptian fields and marshes, where the wild duck cry to each other as they scuttle through the tall reeds. Here in the early morning comes our songstress, and one may see her as clearly as one can that Shulamite of King Solomon's day, who has had the good fortune to belong to a land where stones and bones, being few in number, do not endanger the atmosphere of the literature. One may see her, her hair moving in the breeze "as a flock of goats that appear from Mount Gilead"; her teeth white "as a flock of shorn sheep which came up from the washing," and her lips "like a thread of scarlet." Through such imaginings alone can one appreciate the songs, or realise the lightness of the manner in which they were sung.

With such a happy view of life amongst the upper classes as is indicated by their philosophy, and with that merry disposition amongst the peasants which shows itself in their love of song, it is not surprising to find that asceticism is practically unknown in ancient Egypt before the time of Christ. At first sight, in reflecting on the mysteries and religious ceremonies of the nation, we are apt to endow the priests and other participators with a degree of austerity wholly unjustified by facts. We picture the priest chanting his formulæ in the dim light of the temple, the atmosphere about him heavy with incense; and we imagine him as an anchorite who has put away the things of this world. But in reality there seems to have been not even such a thing as a celibate amongst the priests. Each man had his wife and his family, his house, and his comforts of food and fine linen. He indulged in the usual pastimes and was present at the merriest of feasts. The famous wise men and magicians, such as Uba-ana of the Westcar Papyrus, had their wives, their parks, their pleasure-pavilions, and their hosts of servants. Great dignitaries of the Amon Church, such as Amenhotepsase, the Second Prophet of Amen in the time of Thutmosis IV., are represented as feasting with their friends, or driving through Thebes in richly-decorated chariots drawn by prancing horses, and attended by an array of servants. A monastic life, or the life of an anchorite, was held by the Egyptians in scorn; and indeed the state of mind which produces the monk and the hermit was almost entirely unknown to the nation in dynastic times. It was only in the Ptolemaic and Roman periods that asceticism came to be practised; and some have thought that its introduction into Egypt is to be attributed to the preaching of the Hindoo missionaries sent from India to the court of the Ptolemies. It is not really an Egyptian characteristic; and its practice did not last for more than a few centuries.

The religious teachings of the Egyptians before the Ptolemaic era do not suggest that the mortification of the flesh was a possible means of purifying the spirit. An appeal to the senses and to the emotions, however, was considered as a legitimate method of reaching the soul. The Egyptians were passionately fond of ceremonial display. Their huge temples, painted as they were with the most brilliant colours, formed the setting of processions and ceremonies in which music, rhythmic motion, and colour were brought to a point of excellence. In honour of some of the gods dances were conducted; while celebrations, such as the fantastic Feast of Lamps, were held on the anniversaries of religious events. In these gorgeously spectacular ceremonies there was no place for anything sombre or austere, nor could they have been conceived by any but the most life-loving temperaments.

As in his religious functions, so in his home, the Egyptian regarded brilliancy and festivity as an edification. When in trouble or distress, he was wont to relieve his mind as readily by an appeal to the vanities of this world as by an invocation of the powers of Heaven. Thus, when King Sneferu, of Dynasty IV., was oppressed with the cares of state, his councillor Zazamankh constructed for him a pleasure boat which was rowed around a lake by the most beautiful damsels obtainable. And again, when Wenamon, the envoy of Herhor of Dynasty XXI., had fallen into trouble with the pirates of the Mediterranean, his depression was banished by a gift of a dancing-girl, two vessels of wine, a young goat of tender flesh, and a message which read—"Eat and drink, and let not thy heart feel apprehension."

An intense craving for brightness and cheerfulness is to be observed on all sides, and the attempt to cover every action of life with a kind of lustre is perhaps the most apparent characteristic of the race. At all times the Egyptians decked themselves with flowers, and rich and poor alike breathed what they called "the sweet north wind" through a screen of blossoms. At their feasts and festivals each guest was presented with necklaces and crowns of lotus-flowers, and a specially selected bouquet was carried in the hands. Constantly, as the hours passed, fresh flowers were brought to them, and the guests are shown in the tomb paintings in the act of burying their noses in the delicate petals with an air of luxury which even the conventionalities of the draughtsman cannot hide. In the women's hair a flower was pinned which hung down before the forehead; and a cake of ointment, concocted of some sweet-smelling unguent, was so arranged upon the head that, as it slowly melted, it re-perfumed the flower. Complete wreaths of flowers were sometimes worn, and this was the custom as much in the dress of the home as in that of the feast. The common people also arrayed themselves with wreaths of lotuses at all galas and carnivals. The room in which a feast was held was decorated lavishly with flowers. Blossoms crept up the delicate pillars to the roof; garlands twined themselves around the tables and about the jars of wine; and single buds lay in every dish of food. Even the dead were decked in their tombs with a mass of flowers, as though the mourners would hide with the living delights of the earth the misery of the grave.

The Egyptian loved his garden, and filled it with all manner of beautiful flowers. Great parks were laid out by the Pharaohs, and it is recorded of Thutmosis III. that he brought back from his Asiatic campaigns vast quantities of rare plants with which to beautify Thebes. Festivals were held at the season when the flowers were in full bloom, and the light-hearted Egyptian did not fail to make the flowers talk to him, in the imagination, of the delights of life. In one case a fig-tree is made to call to a passing maiden to come into its shade.

> "Come," it says, "and spend this festal day, and tomorrow, and the day after tomorrow, sitting in my shadow. Let thy lover sit

at thy side, and let him drink . . . Thy servants will come with the dinner-things—they will bring drink of every kind, with all manner of cakes, flowers of yesterday and of today, and all kinds of refreshing fruit."

Than this one could hardly find a more convincing indication of the gaiety of the Egyptian temperament. In the eighteenth and nineteenth centuries A.D. the people were so oppressed that any display of luxury was discouraged, and a happy smile brought the tax-gatherer to the door to ascertain whether it was due to financial prosperity. But the carrying of flowers, and other indications of a kind of unworried contentment, are now again becoming apparent on all sides.

PL. IX. A garland of leaves and flowers dating from about B.C. 1000. It was placed upon the neck of a mummy.
—CAIRO MUSEUM.
*[Photo by E. Brugsch Pasha.*

The affection displayed by the Egyptians for bright colours would alone indicate that their temperament was not melancholic. The houses of the rich were painted with colours which would be regarded as crude had they appeared in the Occident, but which are admissible in Egypt where the natural brilliancy of the sunshine and the scenery demands a more extreme colour-scheme in decoration. The pavilions in which the nobles "made a happy day," as they phrased it, were painted with the most brilliant wall-decorations, and the delicately-shaped lotus columns supporting the roof were striped with half a dozen colours, and were hung with streamers of linen. The ceilings and pavements seem to have afforded the artists a happy field for a display of their originality and skill, and it is on these stretches of smooth-plastered surface that gems of Egyptian art are often found. A pavement from the palace of Akhnaton at Tell el Amârna shows a scene in which a cow is depicted frisking through the reeds, and birds are represented flying over the marshes. In the palace of Amenhotep III. at Gurneh there was a ceiling decoration representing a flight of doves, which, in its delicacy of execution and colouring, is not to be classed with the crude forms of Egyptian decoration, but indicates an equally light-hearted temperament in its creator. It is not probable that either bright colours or daintiness of design would emanate from the brains of a sombre-minded people.

Some of the feminine garments worn in ancient Egypt were exceedingly gaudy, and they made up in colour all that they lacked in variety of design. In the Middle and New Empires the robes of the men were as many-hued as their wall decorations, and as rich in composition. One may take as a typical example the costume of a certain priest who lived at the end of Dynasty XVIII. An elaborate wig covers his head; a richly ornamented necklace surrounds his neck; the upper part of his body is clothed in a tunic of gauze-like linen; as a skirt there is swathed around him the most delicately coloured fine linen, one end of which is brought up and thrown gracefully over his arm; decorated sandals cover his feet and curl up over his toes; and in his hand he carries a jewelled wand surmounted by feathers. It would be an absurdity to state that these folds of fine linen hid a heart set on things higher than this world and its vanities. Nor do the objects of daily use found in the tombs suggest any austerity in the Egyptian character. There is no reflection of the Underworld to be looked for in the ornamental bronze mirrors, nor smell of death in the frail perfume pots. Religious abstraction is not to be sought in lotus-formed drinking-cups, and mortification of the body is certainly not practised on golden chairs and soft cushions. These were the objects buried in the tombs of the priests and religious teachers.

The puritanical tendency of a race can generally be discovered by a study of the personal names of the people. The names by which the Egyptians called their children are as gay as they are pretty, and lack entirely the Puritan character. "Eyes-of-love," "My-lady-is-as-gold," "Cool-breeze," "Gold-and-lapis-lazuli," "Beautiful-morning," are Egyptian names very far removed from "Through-trials-and-tribulations-we-enter-into-the-Kingdom-of-Heaven Jones," which is the actual name of a now living scion of a Roundhead family. And the well-known "Praise-God Barebones" has little to do with the Egyptian "Beautiful-Kitten," "Little-Wild-Lion," "I-have-wanted-you," "Sweetheart," and so on.

The nature of the folk-tales is equally indicative of the temperament of a nation. The stories which have come down to us from ancient Egypt are often as frivolous as they are quaint. Nothing delighted the Egyptians more than the listening to a tale told by an expert story-teller; and it is to be supposed that such persons were in as much demand in the old days as they are now. One may still read of the adventures of the Prince who was fated to die by a dog, a snake, or a crocodile; of the magician who made the waters of the lake heap themselves up that he might descend to the bottom dry-shod to recover a lady's jewel; of the fat old wizard who could cut a man's head off and join it again to his body; of the fairy godmothers who made presents to a new-born babe; of the shipwrecked sailor who was thrown up on an island inhabited by serpents with human natures; of the princess in the tower whose lovers spent their days in attempting to climb to her window,—and so on. The stories have no moral, they are not pompous: they are purely amusing, interesting, and romantic. As an example one may quote the story which is told of Prince Setna, the son of Rameses II. This Prince was one day sitting in the court of the temple of Ptah, when he saw a woman pass "beautiful exceedingly, there being no woman of her beauty." There were wonderful golden ornaments upon her, and she was attended by fifty-two persons, themselves of some rank and much beauty. "The hour that Setna saw her, he knew not the place on earth where he was"; and he called to his servants and told them to "go quickly to the place where she is, and learn what comes under her command." The beautiful lady proved finally to be named Tabubna, the daughter of a priest of Bast, the Cat. Setna's acquaintance with her was later of a most disgraceful character; and, from motives which are not clear, she made him murder his own children to please her. At the critical moment, however, when the climax is reached, the old, old joke is played upon the listener, who is told that Setna then woke up, and discovered that the whole affair had been an afternoon dream in the shade of the temple court.

The Egyptians often amused themselves by drawing comic pictures and caricatures, and there is an interesting series still preserved in which animals take the place of human beings, and are shown performing all manner of antics. One sees a cat walking on its hind legs driving a flock of geese, while a wolf carrying a staff and knapsack leads a herd of goats. There is a battle of the mice and cats, and the king of the mice, in his chariot drawn by two dogs, is seen attacking the fortress of the cats. A picture which is worthy of Edward Lear shows a ridiculous hippopotamus seated amidst the foliage of a tree, eating from a table, whilst a crow mounts a ladder to wait upon him. There are caricatures showing women of fashion rouging their faces, unshaven and really amusing old tramps, and so forth. Even upon the walls of the tombs there are often comic pictures, in which one may see little girls fighting and tearing at each others' hair, men tumbling one over another as they play, and the like; and one must suppose that these were the scenes which the owner of the tomb wished to perpetuate throughout the eternity of Death.

The Egyptians took keen delight in music. In the sound of the trumpet and on the well-tuned cymbals they praised God in Egypt as merrily as the Psalmist could wish. The strings and the pipe, the lute and the harp, made music at every festival—religious, national, or private. Plato tells us that "nothing but beautiful forms and fine music was permitted to enter into the assemblies of young people" in Egypt; and he states that music was considered as being of the greatest consequence for its beneficial effects upon youthful minds. Strabo records the fact that music was largely taught in Egypt, and the numbers of musical instruments buried in the tombs or represented in the decorations confirm his statement. The music was scientifically taught, and a knowledge of harmony is apparent in the complicated forms of the instruments. The harps sometimes had as many as twenty-two strings: the long-handled guitars, fitted with three strings, were capable of wide gradations; and the flutes were sufficiently complicated to be described by early writers as "many-toned." The Egyptian did not merely bang a drum with his fist because it made a noise, nor blow blasts upon a trumpet as a means of expressing the inexpressible. He was an educated musician, and he employed the medium of music to encourage his lightness of heart and to render his gaiety more gay.

PL. X. A relief of the Saitic Period, representing an old man playing upon a harp, and a woman beating a drum. Offerings of food and flowers are placed before them.
—ALEXANDRIA MUSEUM.
*[Photo by E. Brugsch Pasha.]*

One sees representations of the women in a rich man's harem amusing themselves by dancing and singing. In the tomb of Ay there is a scene showing the interior of the women's quarters, and here the ladies are shown dancing, playing guitars, feasting, or adorning themselves with their jewellery; while the store-rooms are seen to be filled with all manner of musical instruments, as well as mirrors, boxes of clothes, and articles of feminine use. At feasts and banquets a string band played during the meal, and songs were sung to the accompaniment of the harp. At religious festivals choruses of male and female voices were introduced. Soldiers marched through the streets to the sound of trumpets and drums, and marriage processions and the like were led by a band. At the feasts it was customary for the dancing-girls, who were employed for the amusement of the guests, to perform their dances and to play a guitar or a flute at the same time. One sees representations of girls, their heads thrown back and their long hair flying, merrily twanging a guitar as they skip round the room. In the civil and religious processions many of the participators danced along as though from sheer lightness of heart; and on some occasions even the band footed it down the high-road, circling, jumping, and skipping as they played.

The words for "rejoice" and "dance" were synonymous in the literature of the Egyptians. In early days dancing naturally implied rejoicing, and rejoicing was most easily expressed by dancing. But the Egyptians of the refined periods more often danced to amuse themselves, regarding it, just as we do at the present day, as an exhilaration. Persons of the upper classes, however, did not indulge very freely in it, but preferred to watch the performances of professional dancers. At all banquets dancing was as indispensable as wine, women, and song, and it rather depended on the nature of the wine and women as to whether the guests joined personally in the sport or sat still while the dancers swayed around the room. The professionals were generally women, but sometimes men were employed, and one sees representations of a man performing some difficult solo while a chorus of women sings and marks time by clapping the hands. Men and women danced together on occasions, but as a general rule the

Egyptian preferred to watch the movements of the more graceful sex by themselves. The women sometimes danced naked, to show off the grace of their poses and the suppleness of their muscles; sometimes they were decked with ribbons only; and sometimes they wore transparent dresses made of linen of the finest texture. It was not unusual for them to carry tambourines and castanets with which to beat time to their dances. On the other hand, there were delicate and sober performances, unaccompanied by music. The paintings show some of the poses to have been exceedingly graceful, and there were character dances enacted in which the figures must have been highly dramatic and artistic. For example, the tableau which occurs in one dance, and is called "The Wind," shows two of the dancing-girls bent back like reeds when the wind blows upon them, while a third figure stands over them in protection, as though symbolising the immovable rocks.

But more usually the merry mood of the Egyptians asserted itself, as it so often does at the present day, in a demand for something approaching nearer to buffoonery. The dancers whirled one another about in the wildest manner, often tumbling head over heels on the floor. A trick, attended generally with success, consisted in the attempt by the dancers to balance the body upon the head without the support of the arms. This buffoonery was highly appreciated by the audience which witnessed it; and the banqueting-room must have been full of the noise of riotous mirth. One cannot, indeed, regard a feast as pompous or solemn at which the banging of the tambourines and the click of castanets vied with the clatter of the dishes and the laughter of the guests in creating a general hullabaloo. Let those state who will that the Egyptian was a gloomy individual, but first let them not fail to observe that same Egyptian standing upon his head amidst the roars of laughter of his friends.

Dancing as a religious ceremony is to be found in many primitive countries, and in Egypt it exists at the present day in more than one form. In the days of the Pharaohs it was customary to institute dances in honour of some of the gods, more especially those deities whose concerns were earthy—that is to say, those connected with love, joy, birth, death, fertility, reproduction, and so on. It will be remembered how David danced before the Ark of the Lord, and how his ancestors danced in honour of the golden calf. In Egypt the king was wont to dance before the great god Min of the crops, and at harvest-time the peasants performed their thanksgiving before the figures of Min in this manner. Hathor and Bast, the two great goddesses of pleasure, were worshipped in the dance. Hathor was mistress of sports and dancing, and patron of amusements and mirth, joy and pleasure, beauty and love; and in regard to the happy temperament of the Egyptians, it is significant that this goddess was held in the highest esteem throughout the history of the nation.

Bast was honoured by a festival which for merriment and frivolity could not well be equalled. The festival took place at Bubastis, and is described by Herodotus in the following words:—

> "This is the nature of the ceremony on the way to Bubastis. They go by water, and numerous boats are crowded with persons of both sexes. During the voyage several women strike the cymbals, some men play the flute, the rest singing and clapping their hands. As they pass near a town they bring the boat close to the bank. Some of the women continue to sing and play the cymbals; others cry out as long as they can, and utter mocking jests against the people of the town, who begin to dance, while the former pull up their clothes before them in a scoffing manner. The same is repeated at every town they pass upon the river. Arrived at Bubastis, they celebrate the festival of Bast, sacrificing a great number of victims, and on that occasion a greater consumption of wine takes place than during the whole of the year."

At this festival of Bast half the persons taking part in the celebrations must have become intoxicated. The Egyptians were always given to wine-drinking, and Athenæus goes so far as to say that they were a nation addicted to systematic intemperance. The same writer, on the authority of Hellanicus, states that the vine was cultivated in the Nile valley at a date earlier than that at which it was first grown by any other people; and it is to this circumstance that Dion attributes the Egyptian's love of wine. Strabo and other writers speak of the wines of Egypt as being particularly good, and various kinds emanating from different localities are mentioned. The wines made from grapes were of the red and white varieties; but there were also fruit wines, made from pomegranates and other fruits. In the lists of offerings inscribed on the walls of temples and tombs one sees a large number of varieties recorded—wines from the north, wines from the south, wines provincial, and wines foreign. Beer, made of barley, was also drunk very largely, and this beverage is heartily commended by the early writers. Indeed, the wine and beer-bibber was so common an offender against the dignity of the nation, that every moralist who arose had a word to say against him. Thus, for example, in the Maxims of Ani one finds the moralist writing—

> "Do not put thyself in a beer-house. An evil thing are words reported as coming from thy mouth when thou dost not know that they have been said by thee. When thou fallest thy limbs are broken, and nobody giveth thee a hand. Thy comrades in drink stand up, saying, 'Away with this drunken man.'"

The less thoughtful members of society, however, considered drunkenness as a very good joke, and even went so far as to portray it in their tomb decorations. One sees men carried home from a feast across the shoulders of three of their companions, or ignominiously hauled out of the house by their ankles and the scruff of their neck. In the tomb of

Paheri at El Kab women are represented at a feast, and scraps of their conversation are recorded, such, for instance, as "Give me eighteen cups of wine, for I should love to drink to drunkenness: my inside is as dry as straw." There are actually representations of women overcome with nausea through immoderate drinking, and being attended by servants who have hastened with basins to their assistance. In another tomb-painting a drunken man is seen to have fallen against one of the delicate pillars of the pavilion with such force that it has toppled over, to the dismay of the guests around.

In the light of such scenes as these one may picture the life of an Egyptian in the elder days as being not a little depraved. One sees the men in their gaudy raiment, and the women luxuriously clothed, staining their garments with the wine spilt from the drinking-bowls as their hands shake with their drunken laughter; and the vision of Egyptian solemnity is still further banished at the sight. It is only too obvious that a land of laughter and jest, feasting and carouse, must be situated too near a Pompeian volcano to be capable of endurance, and the inhabitants too purposeless in their movements to avoid at some time or other running into the paths of burning lava. The people of Egypt went merrily through the radiant valley in which they lived, employing all that the gods had given them,—not only the green palms, the thousand birds, the blue sky, the hearty wind, the river and its reflections, but also the luxuries of their civilisation,—to make for themselves a frail feast of happiness. And when the last flowers, the latest empty drinking-cup, fell to the ground, nothing remained to them but that sodden, drunken night of disgrace which shocks one so at the end of the dynastic history, and which inevitably led to the fall of the nation. Christian asceticism came as the natural reaction and Muhammedan strictness followed in due course; and it required the force of both these movements to put strength and health into the people once more.

PL. XI. An Egyptian noble of the Eighteenth Dynasty hunting birds with a boomerang and decoys. He stands in a reed-boat which floats amidst the papyrus clumps, and a cat retrieves the fallen birds. In the boat with him are his wife and son.—FROM A THEBAN TOMB-PAINTING, BRITISH MUSEUM.

One need not dwell, however, on this aspect of the Egyptian temperament. It is more pleasing, and as pertinent to the argument, to follow the old lords of the Nile into the sunshine once more, and to glance for a moment at their sports. Hunting was a pleasure to them, in which they indulged at every opportunity. One sees representations of this with great frequency upon the walls of the tombs. A man will be shown standing in a reed boat which has been pushed in amongst the waving papyrus. A boomerang is in his hand, and his wife by his side helps him to locate the wild duck, so that he may penetrate within throwing-distance of the birds before they rise. Presently up they go with a whir, and the boomerang claims its victims; while all manner of smaller birds dart from amidst the reeds, and gaudy butterflies pass startled overhead. Again one sees the hunter galloping in his chariot over the hard sand of the desert, shooting his arrows at the gazelle as he goes. Or yet again with his dogs he is shown in pursuit of the long-eared Egyptian hare, or of some other creature of the desert. When not thus engaged he may be seen excitedly watching a bullfight, or eagerly judging the merits of rival wrestlers, boxers, and fencers. One may follow him later into the seclusion of his garden, where, surrounded by a wealth of trees and flowers, he plays draughts with his friends, romps with his children, or fishes in his artificial ponds. There is much evidence of this nature to show that the Egyptian was as much given to these healthy amusements as he was to the mirth of the feast. Josephus states that the Egyptians were a people addicted to pleasure, and the evidence brought together in the foregoing pages shows that his statement is to be confirmed. In sincere joy of living they surpassed any other nation of the ancient world. Life was a thing of such delight to the Egyptian, that he shrank equally from losing it himself and from taking it from another. His prayer was that he might live to be a centenarian. In spite of the many wars of the Egyptians, there was less unnecessary bloodshed in the Nile valley than in any other country which called itself civilised. Death was as terrible to them as it was inevitable, and the constant advice of the thinker was that the living should make the most of their life. When a king died, it was said that "he went forth to heaven having spent life in happiness," or that "he rested after life, having completed his years in happiness." It is true that the Egyptians wished to picture the after-life as one of continuous joy. One sees representations of a man's soul seated in the shade of the fruit-trees of the Underworld, while birds sing in the branches above him, and a lake of cool water lies before him; but they seemed to know that this was too pleasant a picture to be the real one. A woman, the wife of a high priest, left upon her tombstone the following inscription, addressed to her husband:—

> "O, brother, husband, friend," she says, "thy desire to drink and to eat hath not ceased. Therefore be drunken, enjoy the love of women—make holiday. Follow thy desire by night and by day. Put not care within thy heart. Lo! are not these the years of thy life upon earth? For as for the Underworld, it is a land of slumber and heavy darkness, a resting-place for those who have passed within it. Each sleepeth there in his own form, they never awake to see their fellows, they behold not their fathers nor their mothers, their heart is careless of their wives and children."

She knows that she will be too deeply steeped in the stupor of the Underworld to remember her husband, and unselfishly she urges him to continue to be happy after the manner of his nation. Then, in a passage which rings down the years in its terrible beauty, she tells of her utter despair, lying in the gloomy Underworld, suffocated with the mummy bandages, and craving for the light, the laughter, and the coolness of the day.

> "The water of life," she cries, "with which every mouth is moistened, is corruption to me, the water that is by me corrupteth me. I know not what to do since I came into this valley. Give me running water, say to me, 'Water shall not cease to be brought to thee.' Turn my face to the north wind upon the edge of the water. Verily thus shall my heart be cooled and refreshed from its pain."

It is, however, the glory of life, rather than the horror of death, which is the dominant note in the inscriptions and reliefs. The scenes in the tomb decorations seem to cry out for very joy. The artist has imprisoned in his representations as much sheer happiness as was ever infused into cold stone. One sees there the gazelle leaping over the hills as the sun rises, the birds flapping their wings and singing, the wild duck rising from the marshes, and the butterflies flashing overhead. The fundamental joy of living—that gaiety of life which the human being may feel in common with the animals—is shown in these scenes as clearly as is the merriment in the representations of feasts and dancing. In these paintings and reliefs one finds an exact illustration to the joyful exhortation of the Psalmist as he cries, "Let the heavens rejoice, and let the earth be glad; . . . let the fields be joyful, and all that is therein." In a land where, to quote one of their own poems, "the tanks are full of water and the earth overflows with love," where "the cool north wind" blows merrily over the fields, and the sun never ceases to shine, it would be a remarkable phenomenon if the ancient Egyptians had not developed the sanguine temperament. The foregoing pages have shown them at their feasts, in their daily occupations, and in their sports, and the reader will find that it is not difficult to describe them, in the borrowed words of the old geographer, as a people always gay and often frivolous, and never-ceasingly "fond of dancing and red wine."

# CHAPTER V.

## THE MISFORTUNES OF WENAMON.

In the third chapter of this book it has been shown that the archæologist is, to some extent, enamoured of the Past because it can add to the stock of things which are likely to tickle the fancy. So humorous a man is he, so fond of the good things of life, so stirred by its adventures, so touched by its sorrows, that he must needs go to the Past to replenish his supplies, as another might go to Paris or Timbuctoo.

Here, then, is the place to give an example of the entertainment which he is likely to find in this province of his; and if the reader can detect any smell of dust or hear any creak of dead bones in the story which follows, it will be a matter of surprise to me.

In the year 1891, at a small village in Upper Egypt named El Hibeh, some natives unearthed a much damaged roll of papyrus which appeared to them to be very ancient. Since they had heard that antiquities have a market value they did not burn it along with whatever other scraps of inflammable material they had collected for their evening fire, but preserved it, and finally took it to a dealer, who gave them in exchange for it a small sum of money. From the dealer's hands it passed into the possession of Monsieur Golenischeff, a Russian Egyptologist, who happened at the time to be travelling in Egypt; and by him it was carried to St Petersburg, where it now rests. This *savant* presently published a translation of the document, which at once caused a sensation in the Egyptological world; and during the next few years four amended translations were made by different scholars. The interest shown in this tattered roll was due to the fact that it had been found to contain the actual report written by an official named Wenamon to his chief, the High Priest of Amon-Ra, relating his adventures in the Mediterranean while procuring cedar-wood from the forests of Lebanon. The story which Wenamon tells is of the greatest value to Egyptology, giving as it does a vivid account of the political conditions obtaining in Syria and Egypt during the reign of the Pharaoh Rameses XII.; but it also has a very human interest, and the misfortunes of the writer may excite one's sympathy and amusement, after this lapse of three thousand years, as though they had occurred at the present time.

In the time at which Wenamon wrote his report Egypt had fallen on evil days. A long line of incapable descendants of the great Rameses II. and Rameses III. had ruled the Nile valley; and now a wretched ghost of a Pharaoh, Rameses XII., sat upon the throne, bereft of all power, a ruler in name only. The government of the country lay in the hands of two great nobles: in Upper Egypt, Herhor, High Priest of Amon-Ra, was undisputed master; and in Lower Egypt, Nesubanebded, a prince of the city of Tanis (the Zoan of the Bible), virtually ruled as king of the Delta. Both these persons ultimately ascended the throne of the Pharaohs; but at the time of Wenamon's adventures the High Priest was the more powerful of the two, and could command the obedience of the northern ruler, at any rate in all sacerdotal matters. The priesthood of Amon-Ra was the greatest political factor in Egyptian life. That god's name was respected even in the courts of Syria, and though his power was now on the wane, fifty years previously the great religious body which bowed the knee to him was feared throughout all the countries neighbouring to Egypt. The main cause of Wenamon's troubles was the lack of appreciation of this fact that the god's influence in Syria was not as great as it had been in the past; and this report would certainly not have been worth recording here if he had realised that prestige is, of all factors in international relations, the least reliable.

In the year 1113 B.C. the High Priest undertook the construction of a ceremonial barge in which the image of the god might be floated upon the sacred waters of the Nile during the great religious festivals at Thebes; and for this purpose he found himself in need of a large amount of cedar-wood of the best quality. He therefore sent for Wenamon, who held the sacerdotal title of "Eldest of the Hall of the Temple of Amon," and instructed him to proceed to the Lebanon to procure the timber. It is evident that Wenamon was no traveller, and we may perhaps be permitted to picture him as a rather portly gentleman of middle age, not wanting either in energy or pluck, but given, like some of his countrymen, to a fluctuation of the emotions which would jump him from smiles to tears, from hope to despair, in a manner amazing to any but an Egyptian. To us he often appears as an overgrown baby, and his misfortunes have a farcical nature which makes its appeal as much through the medium of one's love of the ludicrous as through that of one's interest in the romance of adventure. Those who are acquainted with Egypt will see in him one of the types of naif, delightful children of the Nile, whose decorous introduction into the parlour of the nations of today is requiring such careful rehearsal.

For his journey the High Priest gave Wenamon a sum of money, and as credentials he handed him a number of letters addressed to Egyptian and Syrian princes, and intrusted to his care a particularly sacred little image of Amon-Ra, known as Amon-of-the-Road, which had probably accompanied other envoys to the Kingdoms of the Sea in times past, and would be recognised as a token of the official nature of any embassy which carried it.

Thus armed Wenamon set out from El Hibeh—probably the ancient Hetbennu, the capital of the Eighteenth Province of Upper Egypt—on the sixteenth day of the eleventh month of the fifth year of the reign of Rameses XII. (1113 B.C.), and travelled down the Nile by boat to Tanis, a distance of some 200 miles. On his arrival at this fair city of the Delta, whose temples and palaces rose on the borders of the swamps at the edge of the sea, Wenamon made his way to the palace of Nesubanebded, and handed to him the letters which he had received from the High Priest. These were caused to be read aloud; and Nesubanebded, hearing that Wenamon was desirous of reaching the Lebanon as soon as possible, made the necessary arrangements for his immediate despatch upon a vessel which happened then to be lying at the quay under the command of a Syrian skipper named Mengebet, who was about to set out for the Asiatic coast. On the first day of the twelfth month, that is to say fourteen days after his departure from his native town, Wenamon set sail from Tanis, crossing the swamps and heading out into "the Great Syrian Sea."

The voyage over the blue rippling Mediterranean was calm and prosperous as the good ship sailed along the barren shores of the land of the Shasu, along the more mountainous coast of Edom, and thence northwards past the cities of Askalon and Ashdod. To Wenamon, however, the journey was fraught with anxiety. He was full of fears as to his reception in Syria, for the first of his misfortunes had befallen him. Although he had with him both money and the image of Amon-of-the-Road, in the excitement and hurry of his departure he had entirely forgotten to obtain again the bundle of letters of introduction which he had given Nesubanebded to read; and thus there were grave reasons for supposing that his mission might prove a complete failure. Mengebet was evidently a stern old salt who cared not a snap of the fingers for Amon or his envoy, and whose one desire was to reach his destination as rapidly as wind and oars would permit; and it is probable that he refused bluntly to return to Tanis when Wenamon informed him of the oversight. This and the inherent distrust of an Egyptian for a foreigner led Wenamon to regard the captain and his men with suspicion; and one must imagine him seated in the rough deck-cabin gloomily guarding the divine image and his store of money. He had with him a secretary and probably two or three servants; and one may picture these unfortunates anxiously watching the Syrian crew as they slouched about the deck. It is further to be remembered that, as a general rule, the Egyptians are most extremely bad sailors.

After some days the ship arrived at the little city of Dor, which nestled at the foot of the Ridge of Carmel; and here they put in to replenish their supplies. Wenamon states in his report that Dor was at this time a city of the Thekel or Sicilians, some wandering band of sea-rovers having left their native Sicily to settle here, at first under the protection of the Egyptians, but now independent of them. The King of Dor, by name Bedel, hearing that an envoy of the High Priest of Amon-Ra had arrived in his harbour, very politely sent down to him a joint of beef, some loaves of bread, and a jar of wine, upon which Wenamon must have set to with an appetite, after subsisting upon the scanty rations of the sea for so long a time.

It may be that the wine was more potent than that to which the Egyptian was accustomed; or perhaps the white buildings of the city, glistening in the sunlight, and the busy quays, engrossed his attention too completely: anyhow, the second of his misfortunes now befel him. One of the Syrian sailors seized the opportunity to slip into his cabin and to steal the money which was hidden there. Before Wenamon had detected the robbery the sailor had disappeared for ever amidst the houses of Dor. That evening the distracted envoy, seated upon the floor of his cabin, was obliged to chronicle the list of stolen money, which list was afterwards incorporated in his report in the following manner:—

| | | |
|---|---|---|
| One vessel containing gold amounting to | 5 | debens, |
| Four vessels containing silver amounting to | 20 | " |
| One wallet containing silver amounting to | 11 | " |
| Total of what was stolen: gold, 5 debens; silver, | 31 | debens. |

A deben weighed about 100 grammes, and thus the robber was richer by 500 grammes of gold, which in those days would have the purchasing value of about £600 in our money, and 3100 grammes of silver, equal to about £2200.[1]

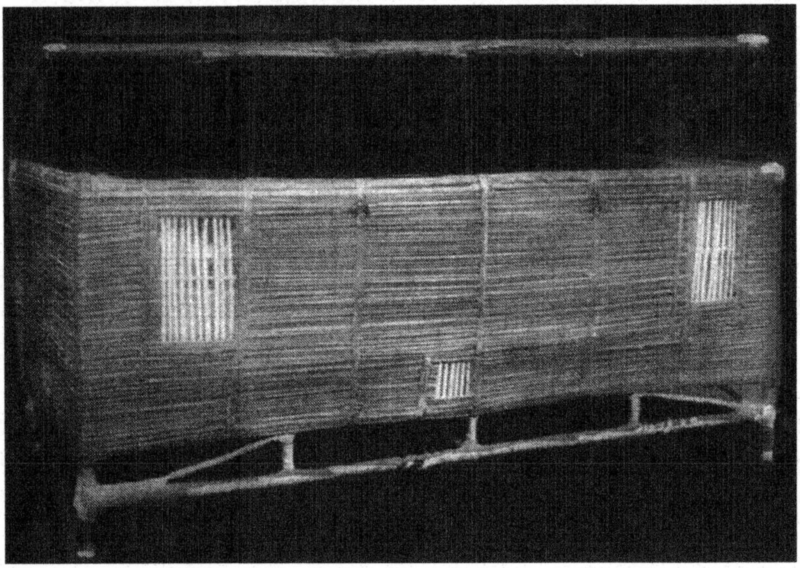

PL. XII. A reed box for holding clothing, discovered in the tomb of Yuaa and Tuau.—CAIRO MUSEUM.
*[Photo by E. Brugsch Pasha.]*

Wenamon must have slept little that night, and early on the following morning he hastened to the palace of King Bedel to lay his case before him. Fortunately Bedel did not ask him for his credentials, but with the utmost politeness he gave his consideration to the affair. Wenamon's words, however, were by no means polite, and one finds in them a blustering assurance which suggests that he considered himself a personage of extreme consequence, and regarded a King of Dor as nothing in comparison with an envoy of Amon-Ra.

1 See Weigall: Catalogue of Weights and Balances in the Cairo Museum, p. xvi.

"I have been robbed in your harbour," he cried, so he tells us in the report, "and, since you are the king of this land, you must be regarded as a party to the crime. You must search for my money. The money belongs to Nesubanebded, and it belongs to Herhor, my lord" (no mention, observe, of the wretched Rameses XII.), "and to the other nobles of Egypt. It belongs also to Weret, and to Mekmel, and to Zakar-Baal the Prince of Byblos."[1] These latter were the persons to whom it was to be paid.

The King of Dor listened to this outburst with Sicilian politeness, and replied in the following very correct terms: "With all due respect to your honour and excellency," he said, "I know nothing of this complaint which you have lodged with me. If the thief belonged to my land and went on board your ship in order to steal your money, I would advance you the sum from my treasury while they were finding the culprit. But the thief who robbed you belonged to your ship. Tarry, however, a few days here with me and I will seek him."

Wenamon, therefore, strode back to the vessel, and there remained, fuming and fretting, for nine long days. The skipper Mengebet, however, had no reason to remain at Dor, and seems to have told Wenamon that he could wait no longer. On the tenth day, therefore, Wenamon retraced his steps to the palace, and addressed himself once more to Bedel. "Look," he said to the king, when he was ushered into the royal presence, "you have not found my money, and therefore you had better let me go with my ship's captain and with those . . ." The rest of the interview is lost in a lacuna, and practically the only words which the damaged condition of the papyrus permits one now to read are, "He said, 'Be silent!'" which indicates that even the patience of a King of Dor could be exhausted.

When the narrative is able to be resumed one finds that Wenamon has set sail from the city, and has travelled along the coast to the proud city of Tyre, where he arrived one afternoon penniless and letterless,

1 The translation is based on that of Prof. Breasted.

having now nothing left but the little Amon-of-the-Road and his own audacity. The charms of Tyre, then one of the great ports of the civilised world, were of no consequence to the destitute Egyptian, nor do they seem to have attracted the skipper of his ship, who, after his long delay at Dor, was in no mood to linger. At dawn the next morning, therefore, the journey was continued, and once more an unfortunate lacuna interrupts the passage of the report. From the tattered fragments of the writing, however, it seems that at the next port of call—perhaps the city of Sidon—a party of inoffensive Sicilian merchants was encountered, and immediately the desperate Wenamon hatched a daring plot. By this time he had come to place some trust in Mengebet, the skipper, who, for the sake of his own good standing in Egypt, had shown himself willing to help the envoy of Amon-Ra in his troubles, although he would not go so far as to delay his journey for him; and Wenamon therefore admitted him to his councils. On some pretext or other a party led by the Egyptian paid a visit to these merchants and entered into conversation with them. Then, suddenly overpowering them, a rush was made for their cash-box, which Wenamon at once burst open. To his disappointment he found it to contain only thirty-one debens of silver, which happened to be precisely the amount of silver, though not of gold, which he had lost. This sum he pocketed, saying to the struggling merchants as he did so, "I will take this money of yours, and will keep it until you find my money. Was it not a Sicilian who stole it, and no thief of ours? I will take it."

With these words the party raced back to the ship, scrambled on board, and in a few moments had hoisted sail and were scudding northwards towards Byblos, where Wenamon proposed to throw himself on the mercy of Zakar-Baal, the prince of that city. Wenamon, it will be remembered, had always considered that he had been robbed by a Sicilian of Dor, notwithstanding the fact that only a sailor of his own ship could have known of the existence of the money, as King Bedel seems to have pointed out to him. The Egyptian, therefore, did not regard this forcible seizure of silver from these other Sicilians as a crime. It was a perfectly just appropriation of a portion of the funds which belonged to him by rights. Let us imagine ourselves robbed at our hotel by Hans the German waiter: it would surely give us the most profound satisfaction to take Herr Schnupfendorff, the piano-tuner, by the throat when next he visited us, and go through his pockets. He and Hans, being of the same nationality, must suffer for one another's sins, and if the magistrate thinks otherwise he must be regarded as prejudiced by too much study of the law.

Byblos stood at the foot of the hills of Lebanon, in the very shadow of the great cedars, and it was therefore Wenamon's destination. Now, however, as the ship dropped anchor in the harbour, the Egyptian realised that his mission would probably be fruitless, and that he himself would perhaps be flung into prison for illegally having in his possession the famous image of the god to which he could show no written right. Moreover, the news of the robbery of the merchants might well have reached Byblos overland. His first action, therefore, was to conceal the idol and the money; and this having been accomplished he sat himself down in his cabin to await events.

The Prince of Byblos certainly had been advised of the robbery; and as soon as the news of the ship's arrival was reported to him he sent a curt message to the captain saying simply, "Get out of my harbour." At this Wenamon gave up all hope, and, hearing that there was then in port a vessel which was about to sail for Egypt, he sent a pathetic message to the prince asking whether he might be allowed to travel by it back to his own country.

No satisfactory answer was received, and for the best part of a month Wenamon's ship rode at anchor, while the distracted envoy paced the deck, vainly pondering upon a fitting course of action. Each morning the same brief order, "Get out of my harbour," was delivered to him by the harbour-master; but the indecision of the authorities as to how to treat this Egyptian official prevented the order being backed by force. Meanwhile Wenamon and Mengebet judiciously spread through the city the report of the power of Amon-of-the-Road, and hinted darkly at the wrath which would ultimately fall upon the heads of those who suffered the image and its keeper to be turned away from the quays of Byblos. No doubt, also, a portion of the stolen debens of silver was expended in bribes to the priests of the city, for, as we shall presently see, one of them took up Wenamon's cause with the most unnatural vigour.

All, however, seemed to be of no avail, and Wenamon decided to get away as best he could. His worldly goods were quietly transferred to the ship which was bound for the Nile; and, when night had fallen, with Amon-of-the-Road tucked under his arm, he hurried along the deserted quay. Suddenly out of the darkness there appeared a group of figures, and Wenamon found himself confronted by the stalwart harbour-master and his police. Now, indeed, he gave himself up for lost. The image would be taken from him, and no longer would he have the alternative of leaving the harbour. He must have groaned aloud as he stood there in the black night, with the cold sea wind threatening to tear the covers from the treasure under his arm. His surprise, therefore, was unbounded when the harbour-master addressed him in the following words: "Remain until morning here near the prince."

The Egyptian turned upon him fiercely. "Are you not the man who came to me every day saying, "Get out of my harbour?" he cried. "And now are you not saying, 'Remain in Byblos?' your object being to let this ship which I have found depart for Egypt without me, so that you may come to me again and say, 'Go away.'"

The harbour-master in reality had been ordered to detain Wenamon for quite another reason. On the previous day, while the prince was sacrificing to his gods, one of the noble youths in his train, who had probably seen the colour of Wenamon's debens, suddenly broke into a religious frenzy, and so continued all that day, and far into the night, calling incessantly upon those around him to go and fetch the envoy of Amon-Ra and the sacred image. Prince Zakar-Baal had considered it prudent to obey this apparently divine command, and had sent the harbour-master to prevent Wenamon's departure. Finding, however, that the Egyptian was determined to board the ship, the official sent a messenger to the prince, who replied with an order to the skipper of the vessel to remain that night in harbour.

Upon the following morning a deputation, evidently friendly, waited on Wenamon, and urged him to come to the palace, which he finally did, incidentally attending on his way the morning service which was being celebrated upon the sea-shore. "I found the prince," writes Wenamon in his report, "sitting in his upper chamber, leaning his back against a window, while the waves of the Great Syrian Sea beat against the wall below. I said to him, 'The mercy of Amon be with you!' He said to me, 'How long is it from now since you left the abode of Amon?' I replied, 'Five months and one day from now.'"

The prince then said, "Look now, if what you say is true, where is the writing of Amon which should be in your hand? Where is the letter of the High Priest of Amon which should be in your hand?"

"I gave them to Nesubanebded," replied Wenamon.

"Then," says Wenamon, "he was very wroth, and he said to me, 'Look here, the writings and the letters are not in your hand. And where is the fine ship which Nesubanebded would have given you, and where is its picked Syrian crew? He would not put you and your affairs in the charge of this skipper of yours, who might have had you killed and thrown into the sea. Whom would they have sought the god from then?—and you, whom would they have sought you from then?' So said he to me, and I replied to him, 'There are indeed Egyptian ships and Egyptian crews that sail under Nesubanebded, but he had at the time no ship and no Syrian crew to give me.'"

The prince did not accept this as a satisfactory answer, but pointed out that there were ten thousand ships sailing between Egypt and Syria, of which number there must have been one at Nesubanebded's disposal.

"Then," writes Wenamon, "I was silent in this great hour. At length he said to me, 'On what business have you come here?' I replied, 'I have come to get wood for the great and august barge of Amon-Ra, king of the gods. Your father supplied it, your grandfather did so, and you too shall do it.' So spoke I to him."

The prince admitted that his fathers had sent wood to Egypt, but he pointed out that they had received proper remuneration for it. He then told his servants to go and find the old ledger in which the transactions were recorded, and this being done, it was found that a thousand debens of silver had been paid for the wood. The prince now argued that he was in no way the servant of Amon, for if he had been he would have been obliged to supply the wood without remuneration. "I am," he proudly declared, "neither your servant nor the servant of him who sent you here. If I cry out to the Lebanon the heavens open and the logs lie here on the shore of the sea." He went on to say that if, of his condescension, he now procured the timber Wenamon would have to provide the ships and all the tackle. "If I make the sails of the ships for you," said the prince, "they may be top-heavy and may break, and you will perish in the sea when Amon thunders in heaven; for skilled workmanship comes only from Egypt to reach my place of abode." This seems to have upset the composure of Wenamon to some extent, and the prince took advantage of his uneasiness to say, "Anyway, what is this miserable expedition that they have had you make (without money or equipment)?"

At this Wenamon appears to have lost his temper. "O guilty one!" he said to the prince, "this is no miserable expedition on which I am engaged. There is no ship upon the Nile which Amon does not own, and his is the sea, and his this Lebanon of which you say, 'It is mine.' Its forests grow for the barge of Amon, the lord of every ship. Why Amon-Ra himself, the king of the gods, said to Herhor, my lord, 'Send me'; and Herhor made me go bearing the statue of this great god. Yet see, you have allowed this great god to wait twenty-nine days after he had arrived in your harbour, although you certainly knew he was there. He is indeed still what he once was: yes, now while you stand bargaining for the Lebanon with Amon its lord. As for Amon-Ra, the king of the gods, he is the lord of life and health, and he was the lord of your fathers, who spent their lifetime offering to him. You also, you are the servant of Amon. If you will say to Amon, 'I will do this,' and you execute his command, you shall live and be prosperous and be healthy, and you shall be popular with your whole country and people. Wish not for yourself a thing belonging to Amon-Ra, king of the gods. Truly the lion loves his own! Let my secretary be brought to me that I may send him to Nesubanebded, and he will send you all that I shall ask him to send, after which, when I return to the south, I will send you all, all your trifles again."

"So spake I to him," says Wenamon in his report, as with a flourish of his pen he brings this fine speech to an end. No doubt it would have been more truthful in him to say, "So would I have spoken to him had I not been so flustered"; but of all types of lie this is probably the most excusable. At all events, he said sufficient to induce the prince to send his secretary to Egypt; and as a token of good faith Zakar-Baal sent with him seven logs of cedar-wood. In forty-eight days' time the messenger returned, bringing with him five golden and five silver vases, twenty garments of fine linen, 500 rolls of papyrus, 500 ox-hides, 500 coils of rope, twenty measures of lentils, and five measures of dried fish. At this present the prince expressed himself most satisfied, and immediately sent 300 men and 300 oxen with proper overseers to start the work of felling the trees. Some eight months after leaving Tanis, Wenamon's delighted eyes gazed upon the complete number of logs lying at the edge of the sea, ready for shipment to Egypt.

The task being finished, the prince walked down to the beach to inspect the timber, and he called to Wenamon to come with him. When the Egyptian had approached, the prince pointed to the logs, remarking that the work had been carried through although the remuneration had not been nearly so great as that which his fathers had received. Wenamon was about to reply when inadvertently the shadow of the prince's umbrella fell upon his head. What memories or anticipations this trivial incident aroused one cannot now tell with certainty. One of the gentlemen-in-waiting, however, found cause in it to whisper to Wenamon, "The shadow of Pharaoh, your lord, falls upon you"—the remark, no doubt, being accompanied by a sly dig in the ribs. The prince angrily snapped, "Let him alone"; and, with the picture of Wenamon gloomily staring out to sea, we are left to worry out the meaning of the occurrence. It may be that the prince intended to keep Wenamon at Byblos until the uttermost farthing had been extracted from Egypt in further payment for the wood, and that therefore he was to be regarded henceforth as Wenamon's king and master. This is perhaps indicated by the following remarks of the prince.

"Do not thus contemplate the terrors of the sea," he said to Wenamon. "For if you do that you should also contemplate my own. Come, I have not done to you what they did to certain former envoys. They spent seventeen years in this land, and they died where they were." Then, turning to an attendant, "Take him," he said, "and let him see the tomb in which they lie."

"Oh, don't let me see it," Wenamon tells us that he cried in anguish; but, recovering his composure, he continued in a more valiant strain. "Mere human beings," he said, "were the envoys who were then sent. There was no god among them (as there now is)."

The prince had recently ordered an engraver to write a commemorative inscription upon a stone tablet recording the fact that the king of the gods had sent Amon-of-the-Road to Byblos as his divine messenger and Wenamon as his human messenger, that timber had been asked for and supplied, and that in return Amon had promised him ten thousand years of celestial life over and above that of ordinary persons. Wenamon now reminded him of this, asking him why he should talk so slightingly of the Egyptian envoys when the making of this tablet showed that in reality he considered their presence an honour. Moreover, he pointed out that when in future years an envoy from Egypt should read this tablet, he would of course pronounce at once the magical prayers which would procure for the prince, who would probably then be in hell after all, a draught of water. This remark seems to have tickled the prince's fancy, for he gravely acknowledged its value, and spoke no more in his former strain. Wenamon closed the interview by promising that the High Priest of Amon-Ra would fully reward him for his various kindnesses.

Shortly after this the Egyptian paid another visit to the sea-shore to feast his eyes upon the logs. He must have been almost unable to contain himself in the delight and excitement of the ending of his task and his approaching return, in triumph to Egypt; and we may see him jauntily walking over the sand, perhaps humming a tune to himself. Suddenly he observed a fleet of eleven ships sailing towards the town, and the song must have died upon his lips. As they drew nearer he saw to his horror that they belonged to the Sicilians of Dor, and we must picture him biting his nails in his anxiety as he stood amongst the logs. Presently they were within hailing distance, and some one called to them asking their business. The reply rang across the water, brief and terrible; "Arrest Wenamon! Let not a ship of his pass to Egypt." Hearing these words the envoy of Amon-Ra, king of the gods, just now so proudly boasting, threw himself upon the sand and burst into tears.

The sobs of the wretched man penetrated to a chamber in which the prince's secretary sat writing at the open window, and he hurried over to the prostrate figure. "Whatever is the matter with you?" he said, tapping the man on the shoulder.

Wenamon raised his head, "Surely you see these birds which descend on Egypt," he groaned. "Look at them! They have come into the harbour, and how long shall I be left forsaken here? Truly you see those who have come to arrest me."

With these words one must suppose that Wenamon returned to his weeping, for he says in his report that the sympathetic secretary went off to find the prince in order that some plan of action might be formulated. When the news was reported to Zakar-Baal, he too began to lament; for the whole affair was menacing and ugly. Looking out of the window he saw the Sicilian ships anchored as a barrier across the mouth of the harbour, he saw the logs of cedar-wood strewn over the beach, he saw the writhing figure of Wenamon pouring sand and dust upon his head and drumming feebly with his toes; and his royal heart was moved with pity for the misfortunes of the Egyptian.

PL. XIII. A festival scene of singers and dancers from a tomb-painting of Dynasty XVII.—THEBES]
*[Copied by H. Petrie.]*

Hastily speaking to his secretary, he told him to procure two large jars of wine and a ram, and to give them to Wenamon on the chance that they might stop the noise of his lamentations. The secretary and his servants procured these things from the kitchen, and, tottering down with them to the envoy, placed them by his side. Wenamon, however, merely glanced at them in a sickly manner, and then buried his head once more. The failure must have been observed from the window of the palace, for the prince sent another servant flying off for a popular Egyptian lady of no reputation, who happened to be living just then at Byblos in the capacity of a dancing-girl. Presently she minced into the room, very much elated, no doubt, at this indication of the royal favour. The prince at once ordered her to hasten down on to the beach to comfort her countryman. "Sing to him," he said. "Don't let his heart feel apprehension."

Wenamon seemed to have waved the girl aside, and we may picture the prince making urgent signs to the lady from his window to renew her efforts. The moans of the miserable man, however, did not cease, and the prince had recourse to a third device. This time he sent a servant to Wenamon with a message of calm assurance. "Eat and drink," he said, "and let not your heart feel apprehension. You shall hear all that I have to say in the morning." At this Wenamon roused himself, and, wiping his eyes, consented to be led back to his rooms, ever turning, no doubt, to cast nervous glances in the direction of the silent ships of Dor.

On the following morning the prince sent for the leaders of the Sicilians and asked them for what reason they had come to Byblos. They replied that they had come in search of Wenamon, who had robbed some of their countrymen of thirty-one debens of silver. The prince was placed in a difficult position, for he was desirous to avoid giving offence either to Dor or to Egypt from whence he now expected further payment; but he managed to pass out on to clearer ground by means of a simple stratagem.

"I cannot arrest the envoy of Amon in my territory," he said to the men of Dor. "But I will send him away, and you shall pursue him and arrest him."

The plan seems to have appealed to the sporting instincts of the Sicilians, for it appears that they drew off from the harbour to await their quarry. Wenamon was then informed of the scheme, and one may suppose that he showed no relish for it. To be chased across a bilious sea by sporting men of hardened stomach was surely a torture for the damned; but it is to be presumed that Zakar-Baal left the Egyptian some chance of escape. Hastily he was conveyed on board a ship, and his misery must have been complete when he observed that outside the harbour it was blowing a gale. Hardly had he set out into the "Great Syrian Sea" before a terrific storm burst, and in the confusion which ensued we lose sight of the waiting fleet. No doubt the Sicilians put in to Byblos once more for shelter, and deemed Wenamon at the bottom of the ocean as the wind whistled through their own bare rigging.

The Egyptian had planned to avoid his enemies by beating northwards when he left the harbour, instead of southwards towards Egypt; but the tempest took the ship's course into its own hands and drove the frail craft north-westwards towards Cyprus, the wooded shores of which were, in course of time, sighted. Wenamon was now indeed 'twixt the devil and the deep sea, for behind him the waves raged furiously, and before him he perceived a threatening group of Cypriots awaiting him upon the wind-swept shore. Presently the vessel grounded upon the beach, and immediately the ill-starred Egyptian and the entire crew were prisoners in the hands of a hostile mob. Roughly they were dragged to the capital of the island, which happened to be but a few miles distant, and with ignominy they were hustled, wet and bedraggled, through the streets towards the palace of Hetebe, the Queen of Cyprus.

As they neared the building the queen herself passed by, surrounded by a brave company of nobles and soldiers. Wenamon burst away from his captors, and bowed himself before the royal lady, crying as he did so, "Surely there is somebody amongst this company who understands Egyptian." One of the nobles, to Wenamon's joy, replied, "Yes, I understand it."

"Say to my mistress," cried the tattered envoy, "that I have heard even in far-off Thebes, the abode of Amon, that in every city injustice is done, but that justice obtains in the land of Cyprus. Yet see, injustice is done here also this day."

This was repeated to the queen, who replied, "Indeed!—what is this that you say?"

Through the interpreter Wenamon then addressed himself to Hetebe. "If the sea raged," he said, "and the wind drove me to the land where I now am, will you let these people take advantage of it to murder me, I who am an envoy of Amon? I am one for whom they will seek unceasingly. And as for these sailors of the prince of Byblos, whom they also wish to kill, their lord will undoubtedly capture ten crews of yours, and will slay every man of them in revenge."

This seems to have impressed the queen, for she ordered the mob to stand on one side, and to Wenamon she said, "Pass the night . . ."

Here the torn writing comes to an abrupt end, and the remainder of Wenamon's adventures are for ever lost amidst the dust of El Hibeh. One may suppose that Hetebe took the Egyptian under her protection, and that ultimately he arrived once more in Egypt, whither Zakar-Baal had perhaps already sent the timber. Returning to his native town, it seems that Wenamon wrote his report, which for some reason or other was never despatched to the High Priest. Perhaps the envoy was himself sent for, and thus his report was rendered useless; or perhaps our text is one of several copies.

There can be no question that he was a writer of great power, and this tale of his adventures must be regarded as one of the jewels of the ancient Egyptian language. The brief description of the Prince of Byblos, seated with his back to the window, while the waves beat against the wall below, brings vividly before one that far-off scene, and reveals a lightness of touch most unusual in writers of that time. There is surely, too, an appreciation of a delicate form of humour observable in his account of some of his dealings with the prince. It is appalling to think that the peasants who found this roll of papyrus might have used it as fuel for their evening fire; and that, had not a drifting rumour of the value of such articles reached their village, this little tale of old Egypt and the long-lost Kingdoms of the Sea would have gone up to empty heaven in a puff of smoke.

# CHAPTER VI.

## THE STORY OF THE SHIPWRECKED SAILOR.

When the early Spanish explorers led their expeditions to Florida, it was their intention to find the Fountain of Perpetual Youth, tales of its potent waters having reached Peter Martyr as early as 1511. This desire to discover the things pertaining to Fairyland has been, throughout history, one of the most fertile sources of adventure. From the days when the archaic Egyptians penetrated into the regions south of the Cataracts, where they believed that the inhabitants were other than human, and into Pount, the "Land of the Ghosts," the hope of Fairyland has led men to search the face of the earth and to penetrate into its unknown places. It has been the theme of countless stories: it has supplied material for innumerable songs.

And in spite of the circumambulations of science about us, in spite of the hardening of all the tissues of our imagination, in spite of the phenomenal development of the commonplace, this desire for a glimpse of the miraculous is still set deeply in our hearts. The old quest of Fairyland is as active now as ever it was. We still presume, in our unworthiness, to pass the barriers, and to walk upon those paths which lead to the enchanted forests and through them to the city of the Moon. At any moment we are ready to set forth, like Arthur's knights, in search of the Holy Grail.

The explorer who penetrates into Central Africa in quest of King Solomon's mines is impelled by a hope closely akin to that of the Spaniards. The excavator who digs for the buried treasures of the Incas or of the Egyptians is often led by a desire for the fabulous. Search is now being made in the western desert of Egypt for a lost city of burnished copper; and the Anglo-Egyptian official is constantly urged by credulous natives to take camels across the wilderness in quest of a town whose houses and temples are of pure gold. What archæologist has not at some time given ear to the whispers that tell of long-lost treasures, of forgotten cities, of Atlantis swallowed by the sea? It is* not only children who love the tales of Fairyland. How happily we have read Kipling's 'Puck of Pook's Hill,' De la Motte Fouqué's 'Undine,' Kenneth Grahame's 'Wind in the Willows,' or F.W. Bain's Indian stories. The recent fairy plays—Barry's "Peter Pan," Maeterlinck's "Blue Bird," and the like—have been enormously successful. Say what we will, fairy tales still hold their old power over us, and still we turn to them as a relief from the commonplace.

Some of us, failing to find Fairyland upon earth, have transferred it to the kingdom of Death; and it has become the hope for the future. Each Sunday in church the congregation of business men and hard-worked women set aside the things of their monotonous life, and sing the songs of the endless search. To the rolling notes of the organ they tell the tale of the Elysian Fields: they take their unfilled desire for Fairyland and adjust it to their deathless hope of Heaven. They sing of crystal fountains, of streets paved with gold, of meadows dressed with living green where they shall dwell as children who now as exiles mourn. There everlasting spring abides and never-withering flowers; there ten thousand times ten thousand clad in sparkling raiment throng up the steeps of light. Here in the church the most unimaginative people cry aloud upon their God for Fairyland.

"The roseate hues of early dawn,
    The brightness of the day,
The crimson of the sunset sky,
    How fast they fade away!
Oh, for the pearly gates of Heaven,
    Oh, for the golden floor . . ."

They know no way of picturing the incomprehensible state of the future, and they interpret it, therefore, in terms of the fairy tale.

I am inclined to think that this sovereignty of the fairies is beneficial. Fairy tales fill the minds of the young with knowledge of the kindly people who will reward with many gifts those that are charitable to the old; they teach a code of chivalry that brings as its reward the love of the beautiful princess in the tower; they tell of dangers overcome by courage and perseverance; they suggest a contact with nature which otherwise might never be developed. Where angels and archangels overawe by their omnipotence, the microscopic fairies who can sit singing upon a mushroom and dangle from the swaying stem of a bluebell, carry the thoughts down the scale of life to the little and really important things. A sleepy child will rather believe that the Queen of the Fairies is acting sentry upon the knob of the bedpost than that an angel stands at the head of the cot with great wings spread in protection—wings which suggest the probability of claws and a beak to match.

The dragons which can only be slain by the noble knight, the enchantments which can only be broken by the outwitting of the evil witch, the lady who can only be won by perils bravely endured, form the material of moral lessons which no other method of teaching could so impress upon the youthful mind.

And when mature years are attained the atmosphere of Fairyland remains with us. The lost songs of the little people drift through the brain, recalling the infinite possibilities of beauty and goodness which are so slightly out of reach; the forgotten wonder of elfs and brownies suggests itself to us from the heart of flowers and amidst the leaves of trees. The clear depths of the sea take half their charm from the memory of the mermaid's palace; the silence of forests is rich with the expectancy of the Knight of the Golden Plume; the large spaces of kitchens and corridors are hushed for the concealment of Robin Goodfellow.

It is the elusiveness, the enchantment, of Fairyland which, for the mature mind, constitutes its greatest value and charm; it is a man's desire for the realms of Midsummer-night that makes the building of those realms in our childhood so valuable. We are constantly endeavouring to recapture the grace of that intangible kingdom, and the hope of ultimate success retains the elasticity of the mind. Held fast by the stiffened joints of reason and closeted with the gout of science, we are fettered prisoners in the world unless there be the knowledge that something eludes us to lead us on. We know quite well that the fairies do not exist, but at the same time we cannot deny that the elusive atmosphere of Fairyland is one with that of our fondest dreams.

Who has not, upon a grey morning, awakened from sleep with the knowledge that he has passed out from a kingdom of dream more dear than all the realms of real life? Vainly we endeavour to recall the lost details, but only the impression remains. That impression, however, warms the tone of our whole day, and frames our thoughts as it were with precious stones. Thus also it is with the memory of our childhood's idea of Fairyland: the impression is recalled, the brain peers forward, the thoughts go on tiptoe, and we feel that we have caught a glimpse of Beauty. Indeed, the recollection of the atmosphere created in our youthful minds by means of fairy tales is perhaps the most abundant of the sources of our knowledge of Beauty in mature years.

I do not suppose that I am alone in declaring that some of the most tender feelings of childhood are inspired by the misfortunes of the Beast in the story of "Beauty and the Beast"; and the Sleeping Beauty is the first love of many a small boy. Man, from his youth up, craves enchantment; and though the business of life gives him no opportunity for the indulging in day-dreams, there are few of us indeed who have not at some time sought the phantom isles, and sought in vain. There is no stormy night, when the wind moans through the trees, and the moon-rack flies overhead, but takes something of its mystery from the recollection of the enchantments of the dark ages. The sun does not sink into the sea amidst the low-lying clouds but some vague thought is brought to mind of the uncharted island whereon that maiden lies sleeping whose hair is dark as heaven's wrath, and whose breast is white like alabaster in the pathway of the moon. There she lies in the charmed circle under the trees, where none may enter until that hour when some pale, lost mariner shall surprise the secret of the pathway, and, coming suddenly upon her, shall kiss her shadowed lips. Vague, elusive, undefined, as such fancies must be, they yet tinge the thoughts of almost every man at certain moments of his life, and set him searching for the enchantment of bygone days. Eagerly he looks for those

"... Magic casements opening on the foam
Of perilous seas, in fairy lands forlorn";

and it is the fact of their unreality that gives them their haunting value.

The following story, preserved in a papyrus now at St Petersburg, describes a mysterious island whereon there dwelt a monster most lovable and most forlorn: a creature so tenderly drawn, indeed, that the reader will not fail to enthrone him in the little company of the nobility of the kingdom of the fairy tale. Translations of the story by two or three savants have appeared; but the present version, which I give in its literal form, has been prepared especially for this volume by Mr Alan Gardiner; and, coming from him, it may be said to be the last word of the science upon the subject of this difficult text.

The scene with which the story opens is clearly indicated by the introductory sentences, though actually it is not described. A large war-galley had come swinging down the Nile from the land of Wawat in the south, the oars flashing in the Nubian sunlight. On the left the granite rocks of the island of Bigeh towered above the vessel; on the right the island of Philæ, as yet devoid of buildings, rested placidly on the blue waters. Ahead were the docks of Shallal, where the clustered boats lay darkly against the yellow of the desert, and busy groups of figures, loading and unloading cargoes, moved to and fro over the sand. Away to the left, behind Bigeh, the distant roar of the First Cataract could be heard as the waters went rushing down from Nubia across the frontier into Egypt.

The great vessel had just returned from the little-known country of Ethiopia, which bordered the Land of the Ghosts, having its frontiers upon the shores of the sea that encircled the world; and the sailors were all straining their eyes towards these docks which formed the southernmost outpost of Egypt, their home. The greatest excitement prevailed on deck; but in the cabin, erected of vari-coloured cloth in the stern of the vessel, the noble leader of the expedition which was now at its conclusion lay in a troubled sleep, tossing nervously upon his bed. His dreams were all of the terrible ordeal which was before him. He could take no pleasure in his home-coming, for he was driven nigh crazy by the thought of entering the presence of the great Pharaoh himself in order to make his report.

PL. XIV. A sailor of Lower Nubia and his son.
*[Photo by E. Bird.]*

It is almost impossible to realise nowadays the agonies of mind that a man had to suffer who was obliged to approach the incarnation of the sun upon earth, and to crave the indulgence of this god in regard to any shortcomings in the conduct of the affairs intrusted to him. Of all the kings of the earth the Pharaoh was the most terrible, the most thoroughly frightening. Not only did he hold the lives of his subjects in his hand to do with them as he chose, but he also controlled the welfare of their immortal souls; for, being a god, he had dominion over the realms of the dead. To be censured by the Pharaoh was to be excommunicated from the pleasures of this earth and outlawed from the fair estate of heaven. A well-known Egyptian noble named Sinuhe, the hero of a fine tale of adventure, describes himself as petrified with terror when he entered the audience-chamber. "I stretched myself on my stomach," he writes, "and became unconscious before him (the Pharaoh). This god addressed me kindly, but I was as a man overtaken by the twilight: my soul departed, my flesh trembled; my heart was no more in my body that I should know life from death."[1] Similarly another personage writes: "Remember the day of bringing the tribute, when thou passest into the Presence under the window, the nobles on each side before his Majesty, the nobles and ambassadors (?) of all countries. They stand and gaze at the tribute, while thou fearest and shrinkest back, and thy hand is weak, and thou knowest not whether it is death or life that is before thee; and thou art brave (only) in praying to thy gods: 'Save me, prosper me this one time.'"[2]

Of the Pharaoh it is written—

"Thine eye is clearer than the stars of heaven;
Thou seest farther than the sun.
If I speak afar off, thine ear hears;
If I do a hidden deed, thine eye sees it."[3]

Or again—

---

1 Sinuhe, 254-256.

2 Papyrus Koller, 5, 1-4.

3 Anastasi Papyri, 4, 5, 6 ff.

"The god of taste is in thy mouth,
The god of knowledge is in thy heart;
Thy tongue is enthroned in the temple of truth;
God is seated upon thy lips."[1]

To meet face to face this all-knowing, all-seeing, celestial creature, from whom there could be no secrets hid nor any guilt concealed, was an ordeal to which a man might well look forward with utter horror. It was this terrible dread that, in the tale with which we are now concerned, held the captain of this Nubian vessel in agony upon his couch.

As he lay there, biting his finger-nails, one of the ship's officers, himself a former leader of expeditions, entered the cabin to announce their arrival at the Shallal docks.

"Good news, prince," said he cheerfully to his writhing master. "Look, we have reached home. They have taken the mallet and driven in the mooring-post; the ship's cable has been put on land. There is merrymaking and thanksgiving, and every man is embracing his fellow. Our crew has returned unscathed, without loss to our soldiers. We have reached the end of Wawat, we have passed Bigeh. Yes, indeed, we have returned safely; we have reached our own land."

At this the prince seems to have groaned anew, much to the distress of his friend, who could but urge him to pull himself together and to play the man.

"Listen to me, prince," he begged, "for I am one void of exaggeration. Wash yourself, pour water on your fingers."

The wretched, man replied, it would seem, with a repetition of his fears; whereupon the old sailor seems to have sat down by his side and to have given him a word of advice as to how he should behave in the king's presence. "Make answer when you are addressed," he said; "speak to the king with a heart in you; answer without restraint. For it is a man's

1 Kubban stela.

mouth that saves him . . . But do as you will: to talk to you is wearisome (to you)."

Presently the old sailor was seized with an idea. He would tell a story, no matter whether it were strictly true or not, in which his own adventures should be set forth. He would describe how he was wrecked upon an unknown island, how he was saved from death, and how, on his return, he conducted into the Pharaoh's presence. A narration of his own experiences before his sovereign might give heart to his captain, and might effectually lift the intolerable burden of dread from the princely shoulders.

"I will relate to you," he began, "a similar thing which befell me my very self. I was making a journey to the mines of the sovereign . . ."

The prince may here be supposed to have sat up and given gloomy attention to his friend's words, for Egyptians of all ages have loved a good story, and tales of adventures in the south were, in early times, most acceptable. The royal gold mines referred to were probably situated at the southern-most end of the eastern Egyptian desert. To reach them one would take ship from Kossair or some other Red Sea port, sail down the coast to the frontiers of Pount, the modern Somaliland, and then travel inland by caravan. It was a perilous undertaking, and, at the time when this story was written, the journey must have furnished material for amazing yarns.

"I went down on the Great Green Sea," continued the speaker, "in a ship one hundred and fifty cubits[1] in length and forty cubits in breadth, and in it were a hundred and fifty sailors, picked men of Egypt. They scanned the heavens and they scanned the earth, and their hearts were stouter than lions. They foretold the storm or ever it came, and the tempest when as yet it was not."

A storm arose while they were out of sight of land, and rapidly increased in violence, until the waves, according to the very restrained

1 The average cubit was about 20-1/2 inches.

estimate of the narrator, were eight cubits high—that is to say, about thirteen or fourteen feet. To one who was accustomed to the waves of the Nile this would be a great height; and the passage thus suggests that the scribe was an untravelled man. A vessel of 150 cubits, or about 250 feet, in length might have been expected to ride out a storm of this magnitude; but, according to the story, she went to pieces, and the whole ship's company, with the single exception of the teller of the tale, were drowned. The survivor managed to cling to a plank of wood, which was driven by the wind towards the shores of an uncharted island, and here at length he was cast up by the waves.

Not far from the beach there was a small thicket, and to this the castaway hastened, sheltering therein from the fury of the storm. For three days in deep despair he lay hidden, "without a companion," as he said, "save my heart;" but at last the tempest subsided, the sun shone in the heavens once again, and the famished mariner was able to go in search of food, which, to his delight, he found in abundance.

The scene upon which he gazed as he plucked the fruit of the laden trees was most mysterious, and all that he saw around him must have had an appearance not altogether consistent with reality, for, indeed, the island was not real. It had been called into existence, perhaps, at the bidding of some god to relieve the tedium of an eternal afternoon, and suddenly it had appeared, floating upon the blue waters of the ocean. How long it had remained there, how long it would still remain, none could tell, for at any moment the mind of the god might be diverted, and instantly it would dissolve and vanish as would a dream. Beneath the isle the seas moved, and there in the darkness the fishes of the deep, with luminous, round eyes, passed to and fro, nibbling the roots of the trees above them. Overhead the heavens stretched, and around about spread the expanse of the sea upon which no living thing might be seen, save only the dolphins as they leapt into the sunshine and sank again amidst the gleaming spray.

There was abundant vegetation upon the island, but it does not appear to have looked quite real. The fig-trees were heavy with fruit, the vines were festooned from bough to bough, hung with clusters of grapes, and pomegranates were ripe for the plucking. But there seems to have been an unearthliness about them, as though a deep enchantment were upon them. In the tangled undergrowth through which the bewildered sailor walked there lay great melons and pumpkins. The breeze wafted to his nostrils the smell of the incense-trees; and the scent of the flowers, after the storm, must have made every breath he breathed a pleasure of Paradise to him. Moving over the luxuriant ground, he put up flights of wonderful birds which sped towards the interior, red, green, and golden, against the sky. Monkeys chattered at him from the trees, and sprang from branch to branch amidst the dancing flowers. In shadowed pools of clear water fishes were to be seen, gliding amidst the reeds; and amongst the rocks beside the sea the castaway could look down upon the creatures of the deep imprisoned between the tides.

Food in all forms was to hand, and he had but to fill his arms with the good things which Fate had provided. "I found there," he said, "figs, grapes, and all manner of goodly onions; melons and pomegranates were there, and pumpkins of every kind. Fishes were there and fowls: there was nought that was lacking in it. I satisfied myself, and set upon the ground the abundance of that with which my arms were filled. I took the fire-borer and kindled a fire, and made a burnt-offering to the gods."

Seated in the warm sunshine amidst the trees, eating a roast fowl seasoned with onions or some equally palatable concoction, he seems to have found the life of a shipwrecked mariner by no means as distressing as he had anticipated; and the wording of the narrative appears to be so arranged that an impression of comfortable ease and security may surround his sunlit figure. Suddenly, however, all was changed. "I heard," said he, "a sound as of thunder, and I thought it was the waves of the sea." Then "the trees creaked and the earth trembled"; and, like the Egyptian that he was, he went down on his shaking hands and knees, and buried his face in the ground.

At length "I uncovered my face," he declared, "and I found it was a serpent that came, of the length of thirty cubits"—about fifty feet—"and his tail was more than two cubits" in diameter. "His skin was overlaid with gold, and his eyebrows were of real lapis lazuli, and he was exceeding perfect."

"He opened his mouth to me," he continued, "as I lay on my stomach before him, and said to me: 'Who brought thee, who brought thee, little one?—who brought thee? If thou delayest to tell me who brought thee to this island I will cause thee to know thyself (again only) when thou art ashes, and art become that which is not seen'"—that is to say, a ghost.

"'Thus you spoke to me," whispered the old sailor, as though again addressing the serpent, who, in the narration of these adventures, had become once more a very present reality to him, "but I heard it not. I lay before thee, and was unconscious."

Continuing his story, he told how the great serpent lifted him tenderly in his golden mouth, and carried him to his dwelling-place, setting him down there without hurt, amongst the fruit-trees and the flowers. The Egyptian at once flung himself upon his stomach before him, and lay there in a stupor of terror. The serpent, however, meant him no harm, and indeed looked down on him with tender pity as he questioned him once more.

"Who brought thee, who brought thee, little one?" he asked again, "Who brought thee to this island of the Great Green Sea, whereof the (under) half is waves?"

On his hands and knees before the kindly monster the shipwrecked Egyptian managed to regain possession of his faculties sufficiently to give an account of himself.

"I was going down to the mines," he faltered, "on a mission of the sovereign, in a ship one hundred and fifty cubits in length and forty in breadth, and in it were one hundred and fifty sailors, picked men of

Egypt. They scanned the heavens and they scanned the earth, and their hearts were stouter than lions. They foretold the storm or ever it came, and the tempest when as yet it was not. Every one of them, his heart was stout and his arm strong beyond his fellow. There was none unproven amongst them. The storm arose while that we were on the Great Green Sea, before we touched land; and as we sailed it redoubled (its strength), and the waves thereof were eight cubits. There was a plank of wood to which I clung. The ship perished, and of them that were in her not one was left saving me alone, who now am at your side. And I was brought to this island by the waves of the Great Green Sea."

At this point the man seems to have been overcome once more with terror, and the serpent, therefore, hastened to reassure him.

"Fear not, little one," he said in his gentle voice; "fear not. Let not thy face be dismayed. If thou hast come to me it is God who has let thee live, who has brought thee to this phantom isle in which there is naught that is lacking, but it is full of all good things. Behold, thou shalt pass month for month until thou accomplish four months upon this island. And a ship shall come from home, and sailors in it whom thou knowest, and thou shalt go home with them, and shalt die in thine own city."

"How glad is he," exclaimed the old mariner as he related his adventures to the prince, "how glad is he that recounts what he has experienced when the calamity is passed!" The prince, no doubt, replied with a melancholy grunt, and the thread of the story was once more taken up.

There was a particular reason why the serpent should be touched and interested to hear how Providence had saved the Egyptian from death, for he himself had survived a great calamity, and had been saved from an equally terrible fate, as he now proceeded to relate.

"I will tell to thee the like thereof," he said, "which happened in this island. I dwelt herein with my brothers, and my children were among them. Seventy-two serpents we were, all told, with my offspring and my brothers; nor have I yet mentioned to thee a little girl brought to me by fortune. A star came down, and all these went up in the flames.

And it happened so that I was not together with them when they were consumed; I was not in their midst. I could have died (of grief) for them when I found them as a single pile of corpses."

It is clear from the story that this great serpent was intended to be pictured as a sad and lonely, but most lovable, character. All alone upon this ghostly isle, the last of his race, one is to imagine him dreaming of the little girl who was taken from him, together with all his family. Although fabulous himself, and half divine, he was yet the victim of the gods, and was made to suffer real sorrows in his unreal existence. Day by day he wandered over his limited domain, twisting his golden body amidst the pumpkins, and rearing himself above the fig-trees; thundering down to the beach to salute the passing dolphins, or sunning himself, a golden blaze, upon the rocks. There remained naught for him to do but to await the cessation of the phantasy of his life; and yet, though his lot was hard, he was ready at once to subordinate his sorrows to those of the shipwrecked sailor before him. No more is said of his distress, but with his next words he seems to have dismissed his own misfortunes, and to have attempted to comfort the Egyptian.

"If thou art brave," he said, "and restrainest thy longing, thou shalt press thy children to thy bosom and kiss thy wife, and behold thy house—that is the best of all things. Thou shalt reach home, and shalt dwell there amongst thy brothers."

"Thereat," said the mariner, "I cast me upon my stomach and touched the ground before him, and I said to him: 'I will tell of thy might to the Sovereign, I will cause him to be acquainted with thy greatness. I will let bring to thee perfume and spices, myrrh and sweet-scented woods, and incense of the sanctuaries wherewithal every god is propitiated. I will recount all that has befallen me, and that which I have seen by his might; and they shall praise thee in that city before the magistrates of the entire land. I will slaughter to thee oxen as a burnt-offering, geese will I pluck for thee, and I will let bring to thee vessels laden with all the goodly things of Egypt, as may be (fitly) done to a god who loves men in a distant land, a land unknown to men.'"

At these words the serpent opened his golden mouth and fell to laughing. The thought that this little mortal, grovelling before him, could believe himself able to repay the kindnesses received tickled him immensely.

"Hast thou not much incense (here, then)?" he laughed. "Art not become a lord of frankincense? And I, behold I am prince of Pount," the land of perfumes, "and the incense, *that* is my very own. As for the spices which thou sayest shall be brought, they are the wealth of this island. But it shall happen when thou hast left this place, never shalt thou see this island more, for it shall be changed to waves."

The teller of the story does not relate in what manner he received this well-merited reproof. The gentle monster, no doubt, was tolerant of his presumptuousness, and soon put him at his ease again. During the whole period of the Egyptian's residence on the island, in fact, the golden serpent seems to have been invariably kind to him. The days passed by like a happy dream, and the spell of the island's enchantment possessed him so that, in after times, the details of the events of every day were lost in the single illusion of the whole adventure.

At last the ship arrived, as it had been foretold, and the sailor watched her passing over the hazy sea towards the mysterious shore. "I went and got me up into a tall tree," he said, "and I recognised those that were in it. And I went to report the matter (to the serpent), and I found that he knew it."

Very tenderly the great monster addressed him. "Fare thee well, little one," he said "Fare thee well to thy house. Mayest thou see thy children and raise up a good name in thy city. Behold, such are my wishes for thee."

"Then," continued the sailor, "I laid me on my stomach, my arms were bended before him. And he gave me a freight of frankincense, perfume and myrrh, sweet-scented woods and antimony, giraffes' tails, great heaps of incense, elephant tusks, dogs, apes and baboons, and all manner of valuable things. And I loaded them in that ship, and I laid myself on my stomach to make thanksgiving to him. Then he said to me: 'Behold, thou shalt come home in two months, and shalt press thy children to thy bosom, and shalt flourish in their midst; and there thou shalt be buried.'"

PL. XV. A Nile boat passing the hills of Thebes.
*[Photo by E. Bird.]*

To appreciate the significance of these last words it is necessary to remember what an important matter it was to an Egyptian that he should be buried in his native city. In our own case the position upon the map of the place where we lay down our discarded bones is generally not of first-rate importance, and the thought of being buried in foreign lands does not frighten us. Whether our body is to be packed away in the necropolis of our city, or shovelled into a hole on the outskirts of Timbuctoo, is not a matter of vital interest. There is a certain sentiment that leads us to desire interment amidst familiar scenes, but it is subordinated with ease to other considerations. To the Egyptian, however, it was a matter of paramount importance. "What is a greater thing," says Sinuhe in the tale of his adventures in Asia, "than that I should be buried in the land in which I was born?" "Thou shalt not die in a foreign land; Asiatics shall not conduct thee to the tomb," says the Pharaoh to him; and again, "It is no little thing that thou shalt be buried without Asiatics conducting thee."[1] There is a stela now preserved in Stuttgart, in which the deceased man asks those who pass his tomb to say a prayer for his soul; and he adjures them in these words: "So truly as ye wish that your native gods should praise you, and that ye should be established in your seats, and that ye should hand down your offices to your children: that ye should reach your homes in safety, and recount your travels to your wives;—then say a prayer," &c.[2]

The serpent was thus giving the castaway a promise which meant more to him than all the other blessings, and it was with a light heart indeed that he ran down to the beach to greet his countrymen. "I went down to the shore where the ship was," he continued, "and I called to the soldiers which were in that ship, and I gave praises upon the shore to the lord of this island, and likewise did they which were in the ship."

Then he stepped on board, the gangway was drawn up, and, with a great sweep of the oars, the ship passed out on to the open sea. Standing on deck amongst the new cargo, the officers and their rescued friend bowed low to the great serpent who towered above the trees at the water's edge, gleaming in the sunshine. "Fare thee well, little one," his deep voice

1 Sinuhe, B. 159, 197, 258.
2 Zeit. Aeg. Spr., 39 (1901), p. 118.

rolled across the water; and again they bowed in obeisance to him. The main-sail was unfurled to the wind, and the vessel scudded bravely across the Great Green Sea; but for some time yet they must have kept their eyes upon the fair shape of the phantom island, as the trees blended into the hills and the hills at last into the haze; and their vision must have been focussed upon that one gleaming point where the golden serpent, alone once more with his memories, watched the ship moving over the fairy seas.

"So sailed we northwards," said the sailor, "to the place of the Sovereign, and we reached home in two months, in accordance with all that he had said. And I entered in before the Sovereign, and I brought to him this tribute which I had taken away from within this island. Then gave he thanksgivings for me before the magistrates of the entire land. And I was made a 'Follower,' and was rewarded with the serfs of such an one."

The old sailor turned to the gloomy prince as he brought his story to an end. "Look at me," he exclaimed, "now that I have reached land, now that I have seen (again in memory) what I have experienced. Hearken thou to me, for behold, to hearken is good for men."

But the prince only sighed the more deeply, and, with a despairing gesture, replied: "Be not (so) superior, my friend! Doth one give water to a bird on the eve, when it is to be slain on the morrow?" With these words the manuscript abruptly ends, and we are supposed to leave the prince still disconsolate in his cabin, while his friend, unable to cheer him, returns to his duties on deck.

# PART III.

## RESEARCHES IN THE TREASURY.

"... And he, shall be,

Man, her last work, who seem'd so fair,
Such splendid purpose in his eyes,
Who roll'd the psalm to wintry skies,
Who built him fanes of fruitless prayer,

Who loved, who suffered countless ills,
Who battled for the True, the Just,
Be blown about the desert dust,
Or seal'd within the iron hills?"

—TENNYSON.

# CHAPTER VII.

# RECENT EXCAVATIONS IN EGYPT.

There came to the camp of a certain professor, who was engaged in excavating the ruins of an ancient Egyptian city, a young and faultlessly-attired Englishman, whose thirst for dramatic adventure had led him to offer his services as an unpaid assistant digger. This immaculate personage had read in novels and tales many an account of the wonders which the spade of the excavator could reveal, and he firmly believed that it was only necessary to set a "nigger" to dig a little hole in the ground to open the way to the treasuries of the Pharaohs. Gold, silver, and precious stones gleamed before him, in his imagination, as he hurried along subterranean passages to the vaults of long-dead kings. He expected to slide upon the seat of his very well-made breeches down the staircase of the ruined palace which he had entered by way of the skylight, and to find himself, at the bottom, in the presence of the bejewelled dead. In the intervals between such experiences he was of opinion that a little quiet gazelle shooting would agreeably fill in the swiftly passing hours; and at the end of the season's work he pictured himself returning to the bosom of his family with such a tale to tell that every ear would be opened to him.

On his arrival at the camp he was conducted to the site of his future labours; and his horrified gaze was directed over a large area of mud-pie, knee-deep in which a few bedraggled natives slushed their way downwards. After three weeks' work on this distressing site, the professor announced that he had managed to trace through the mud the outline of the palace walls, once the feature of the city, and that the work here might now be regarded as finished. He was then conducted to a desolate spot in the desert, and until the day on which he fled back to England he was kept to the monotonous task of superintending a gang of natives whose sole business it was to dig a very large hole in the sand, day after day and week after week.

It is, however, sometimes the fortune of the excavator to make a discovery which almost rivals in dramatic interest the tales of his youth. Such as experience fell to the lot of Emil Brugsch Pasha when he was lowered into an ancient tomb and found himself face to face with a score of the Pharaohs of Egypt, each lying in his coffin; or again, when Monsieur de Morgan discovered the great mass of royal jewels in one of the pyramids at Dachour. But such "finds" can be counted on the fingers, and more often an excavation is a fruitless drudgery. Moreover, the life of the digger is not often a pleasant one.

PL. XVI. The excavations on the site of the city of Abydos.
*[Photo by the Author.]*

It will perhaps be of interest to the reader of romances to illustrate the above remarks by the narration of some of my own experiences; but there are only a few interesting and unusual episodes in which I have had the peculiarly good fortune to be an actor. There will probably be some drama to be felt in the account of the more important discoveries (for there certainly is to the antiquarian himself); but it should be pointed out that the interest of these rare finds pales before the description, which many of us have heard, of how the archæologists of a past century discovered the body of Charlemagne clad in his royal robes and seated upon his throne,—which, by the way, is quite untrue. In spite of all that is said to the contrary, truth is seldom stranger than fiction; and the reader who desires to be told of the discovery of buried cities whose streets are paved with gold should take warning in time and return at once to his novels.

If the dawning interest of the reader has now been thoroughly cooled by these words, it may be presumed that it will be utterly annihilated by the following narration of my first fruitless excavation; and thus one will be able to continue the story with the relieved consciousness that nobody is attending.

In the capacity of assistant to Professor Flinders Petrie, I was set, many years ago, to the task of excavating a supposed royal cemetery in the desert behind the ancient city of Abydos, in Upper Egypt. Two mounds were first attacked; and after many weeks of work in digging through the sand, the superstructure of two great tombs was bared. In the case of the first of these several fine passages of good masonry were cleared, and at last the burial-chamber was reached. In the huge sarcophagus which was there found great hopes were entertained that the body and funeral-offerings of the dead prince would be discovered; but when at last the interior was laid bare the solitary article found was a copy of a French newspaper left behind by the last, and equally disgusted, excavator. The second tomb defied the most ardent exploration, and failed to show any traces of a burial. The mystery was at last solved by Professor Petrie, who, with his usual keen perception, soon came to the conclusion that the whole tomb was a dummy, built solely to hide an enormous mass of rock chippings the presence of which had been a puzzle for some time. These masons' chippings were evidently the output from some large cutting in the rock, and it became apparent that there must be a great rock tomb in the neighbourhood. Trial trenches in the vicinity presently revealed the existence of a long wall, which, being followed in either direction, proved to be the boundary of a vast court or enclosure built upon the desert at the foot of a conspicuous cliff. A ramp led up to the entrance; but as it was slightly askew and pointed to the southern end of the enclosure, it was supposed that the rock tomb, which presumably ran into the cliff from somewhere inside this area, was situated at that end. The next few weeks were occupied in the tedious task of probing the sand hereabouts, and at length in clearing it away altogether down to the surface of the underlying rock. Nothing was found, however; and sadly we turned to the exact middle of the court, and began to work slowly to the foot of the cliff. Here, in the very middle of the back wall, a pillared chamber was found, and it seemed certain that the entrance to the tomb would now be discovered.

The best men were placed to dig out this chamber, and the excavator—it was many years ago—went about his work with the weight of fame upon his shoulders and an expression of intense mystery upon his sorely sun-scorched face. How clearly memory recalls the letter home that week, "We are on the eve of a great discovery"; and how vividly rises the picture of the baking desert sand into which the sweating workmen were slowly digging their way! But our hopes were short-lived, for it very soon became apparent that there was no tomb entrance in this part of the enclosure. There remained the north end of the area, and on to this all the available men were turned. Deeper and deeper they dug their way, until the mounds of sand thrown out formed, as it were, the lip of a great crater. At last, some forty or fifty feet down, the underlying rock was struck, and presently the mouth of a great shaft was exposed leading down into the bowels of the earth. The royal tomb had at last been discovered, and it only remained to effect an entrance. The days were now filled with excitement, and, the thoughts being concentrated on the question of the identity of the royal occupant of the tomb, it was soon fixed in our minds that we were about to enter the burial-place of no less a personage than the great Pharaoh Senusert III. (Sesostris), the same king whose jewels were found at Dachour.

One evening, just after I had left the work, the men came down to the distant camp to say that the last barrier was now reached and that an entrance could be effected at once. In the pale light of the moon, therefore, I hastened back to the desert with a few trusted men. As we walked along, one of these natives very cheerfully remarked that we should all probably get our throats cut, as the brigands of the neighbourhood got wind of the discovery, and were sure to attempt to enter the tomb that night. With this pleasing prospect before us we walked with caution over the silent desert. Reaching the mound of sand which surrounded our excavation, we crept to the top and peeped over into the crater. At once we observed a dim light below us, and almost immediately an agitated but polite voice from the opposite mound called out in Arabic, "Go away, mister. We have all got guns." This remark was followed by a shot which whistled past me; and therewith I slid down the hill once more, and heartily wished myself safe in my bed. Our party then spread round the crater, and at a given word we proposed to rush the place. But the enemy was too quick for us, and after the briefest scrimmage, and the exchanging* of a harmless shot or two, we found ourselves in possession of the tomb, and were able to pretend that we were not a bit frightened.

*Transcriber's note: Original text read "exhanging".

Then into the dark depths of the shaft we descended, and ascertained that the robbers had not effected an entrance. A long night watch followed, and the next day we had the satisfaction of arresting some of the criminals. The tomb was found to penetrate several hundred feet into the cliff, and at the end of the long and beautifully worked passage the great royal sarcophagus was found—empty! So ended a very strenuous season's work.

If the experiences of a digger in Professor Petrie's camp are to be regarded as typical, they will probably serve to damp the ardour of eager young gentlemen in search of ancient Egyptian treasure. One lives in a bare little hut constructed of mud, and roofed with cornstalks or corrugated iron; and if by chance there happened to be a rain storm, as there was when I was a member of the community, one may watch the frail building gently subside in a liquid stream on to one's bed and books. For seven days in the week one's work continues, and it is only to the real enthusiast that that work is not monotonous and tiresome.

A few years later it fell to my lot to excavate for the Government the funeral temple of Thutmosis III. at Thebes, and a fairly large sum was spent upon the undertaking. Although the site was most promising in appearances, a couple of months' work brought to light hardly a single object of importance, whereas exactly similar sites in the same neighbourhood had produced inscriptions of the greatest value. Two years ago I assisted at an excavation upon a site of my own selection, the net result of which, after six weeks' work, was one mummified cat! To sit over the work day after day, as did the unfortunate promoter of this particular enterprise, with the flies buzzing around his face and the sun blazing down upon him from a relentless sky, was hardly a pleasurable task; and to watch the clouds of dust go up from the tip-heap, where tons of unprofitable rubbish rolled down the hillside all day long, was an occupation for the damned. Yet that is excavating as it is usually found to be.

Now let us consider the other side of the story. In the Valley of the Tombs of the Kings at Thebes excavations have been conducted for some years by Mr Theodore M. Davis, of Newport, Rhode Island, by special arrangement with the Department of Antiquities of the Egyptian Government; and as an official of that Department I have had the privilege of being present at all the recent discoveries. The finding of the tomb of Yuaa and Tuau a few years ago was one of the most interesting archæological events of recent times, and one which came somewhere near to the standard of romance set by the novelists. Yuaa and Tuau were the parents of Queen Tiy, the discovery of whose tomb is recorded in the next chapter. When the entrance of their tomb was cleared, a flight of steps was exposed, leading down to a passage blocked by a wall of loose stones. In the top right-hand corner a small hole, large enough to admit a man, had been made in ancient times, and through this we could look down into a dark passage. As it was too late in the day to enter at once, we postponed that exciting experience until the morrow, and some police were sent for to guard the entrance during the night. I had slept the previous night over the mouth, and there was now no possibility of leaving the place for several more nights, so a rough camp was formed on the spot.

Here I settled myself down for the long watch, and speculated on the events of the next morning, when Mr Davis and one or two well-known Egyptologists were to come to the valley to open the sepulchre. Presently, in the silent darkness, a slight noise was heard on the hillside, and immediately the challenge of the sentry rang out. This was answered by a distant call, and after some moments of alertness on our part we observed two figures approaching us. These, to my surprise, proved to be a well-known American artist and his wife,[1] who had obviously come on the expectation that trouble was ahead; but though in this they were certainly destined to suffer disappointment, still, out of respect for the absolute unconcern of both visitors, it may be mentioned that the mouth of a lonely tomb already said by native rumour to contain incalculable wealth is not perhaps the safest place in the world. Here, then, on a level patch of rock we three lay down and slept fitfully until the dawn. Soon after breakfast the wall at the mouth of the tomb was pulled down, and the party passed into the low passage which sloped down to the burial

1 Mr and Mrs Joseph Lindon Smith.

chamber. At the bottom of this passage there was a second wall blocking the way; but when a few layers had been taken off the top we were able to climb, one by one, into the chamber.

PL. XVII. Excavating the Osireion at Abydos. A chain of boys handing up baskets of sand to the surface.
*[Photo by the Author.]*

Imagine entering a town house which had been closed for the summer: imagine the stuffy room, the stiff, silent appearance of the furniture, the feeling that some ghostly occupants of the vacant chairs have just been disturbed, the desire to throw open the windows to let life into room once more. That was perhaps the first sensation as we stood, really dumfounded, and stared around at the relics of the life of over three thousand years ago, all of which were as new almost as when they graced the palace of Prince Yuaa. Three arm-chairs were perhaps the first objects to attract the attention: beautiful carved wooden chairs, decorated with gold. Belonging to one of these was a pillow made of down and covered with linen. It was so perfectly preserved that one might have sat upon it or tossed it from this chair to that without doing it injury. Here were fine alabaster vases, and in one of these we were startled to find a liquid, like honey or syrup, still unsolidified by time. Boxes of exquisite workmanship stood in various parts of the room, some resting on delicately wrought legs. Now the eye was directed to a wicker trunk fitted with trays and partitions, and ventilated with little apertures, since the scents were doubtless strong. Two most comfortable beds were to be observed, fitted with springy string mattresses and decorated with charming designs in gold. There in the far corner, placed upon the top of a number of large white jars, stood the light chariot which Yuaa had owned in his lifetime. In all directions stood objects gleaming with gold undulled by a speck of dust, and one looked from one article to another with the feeling that the entire human conception of Time was wrong. These were the things of yesterday, of a year or so ago. Why, here were meats prepared for the feasts in the Underworld; here were Yuaa's favourite joints, each neatly placed in a wooden box as though for a journey. Here was his staff, and here were his sandals,—a new pair and an old. In another corner there stood the magical figures by the power of which the prince was to make his way through Hades. The words of the mystical "Chapter of the Flame" and of the "Chapter of the Magical Figure of the North Wall" were inscribed upon them; and upon a great roll of papyrus twenty-two yards in length other efficacious prayers were written.

But though the eyes passed from object to object, they ever returned to the two lidless gilded coffins in which the owners of this room of the dead lay as though peacefully sleeping. First above Yuaa and then above his wife the electric lamps were held, and as one looked down into their quiet faces there was almost the feeling that they would presently open their eyes and blink at the light. The stern features of the old man commanded one's attention, again and again our gaze was turned from this mass of wealth to this sleeping figure in whose honour it had been placed here.

At last we returned to the surface to allow the thoughts opportunity to collect themselves and the pulses time to quiet down, for, even to the most unemotional, a discovery of this kind, bringing one into the very presence of the past, has really an unsteadying effect. Then once more we descended, and made the preliminary arrangements for the cataloguing of the antiquities. It was now that the real work began, and, once the excitement was past, there was a monotony of labour to be faced which put a very considerable strain on the powers of all concerned. The hot days when one sweated over the heavy packing-cases, and the bitterly cold nights when one lay at the mouth of the tomb under the stars, dragged on for many a week; and when at last the long train of boxes was carried down to the Nile *en route* for the Cairo Museum, it was with a sigh of relief that the official returned to his regular work.

This, of course, was a very exceptional discovery. Mr Davis has made other great finds, but to me they have not equalled in dramatic interest the discovery just recorded. Even in this royal valley, however, there is much drudgery to be faced, and for a large part of the season's work it is the excavator's business to turn over endless masses of rock chippings, and to dig huge holes which have no interest for the patient digger. Sometimes the mouth of a tomb is bared, and is entered with the profoundest hopes, which are at once dashed by the sudden abrupt ending of the cutting a few yards from the surface. At other times a tomb-chamber is reached and is found to be absolutely empty.

At another part of Thebes the well-known Egyptologist, Professor Schiaparelli, had excavated for a number of years without finding anything of much importance, when suddenly one fine day he struck the mouth of a large tomb which was evidently intact. I was at once informed of the discovery, and proceeded to the spot as quickly as possible. The mouth of the tomb was approached down a flight of steep, rough steps, still half-choked with *débris*. At the bottom of this the entrance of a passage running into the hillside was blocked by a wall of rough stones. After photographing and removing this, we found ourselves in a long, low tunnel, blocked by a second wall a few yards ahead. Both these walls were intact, and we realised that we were about to see what probably no living man had ever seen before: the absolutely intact remains of a rich Theban of the Imperial Age—*i.e.*, about 1200 or 1300 B.C. When this second wall was taken down we passed into a carefully-cut passage high enough to permit of one standing upright.

At the end of this passage a plain wooden door barred our progress. The wood retained the light colour of fresh deal, and looked for all the world as though it had been set up but yesterday. A heavy wooden lock, such as is used at the present day, held the door fast. A neat bronze handle on the side of the door was connected by a spring to a wooden knob set in the masonry door-post; and this spring was carefully sealed with a small dab of stamped clay. The whole contrivance seemed so modern that Professor Schiaparelli called to his servant for the key, who quite seriously replied, "I don't know where it is, sir." He then thumped the door with his hand to see whether it would be likely to give; and, as the echoes reverberated through the tomb, one felt that the mummy, in the darkness beyond, might well think that his resurrection call had come. One almost expected him to rise, like the dead knights of Kildare in the Irish legend, and to ask, "Is it time?" for the three thousand years which his religion had told him was the duration of his life in the tomb was already long past.

Meanwhile we turned our attention to the objects which stood in the passage, having been placed there at the time of the funeral, owing to the lack of room in the burial-chamber. Here a vase, rising upon a delicately shaped stand, attracted the eye by its beauty of form; and here a bedstead caused us to exclaim at its modern appearance. A palm-leaf fan, used by the ancient Egyptians to keep the flies off their wines and unguents, stood near a now empty jar; and near by a basket of dried-up fruit was to be seen. This dried fruit gave the impression that the tomb was perhaps a few months old, but there was nothing else to be seen which suggested that the objects were even as much as a year old. It was almost impossible to believe, and quite impossible to realise, that we were standing where no man had stood for well over three thousand years; and that we were actually breathing the air which had remained sealed in the passage since the ancient priests had closed the entrance thirteen hundred years before Christ.

Before we could proceed farther, many flashlight photographs had to be taken, and drawings made of the doorway; and after this a panel of the woodwork had to be removed with a fret-saw in order that the lock and seal might not be damaged. At last, however, this was accomplished, and the way into the tomb-chamber was open. Stepping through the frame of the door, we found ourselves in an unencumbered portion of the floor, while around us in all directions stood the funeral furniture, and on our left the coffins of the deceased noble and his wife loomed large. Everything looked new and undecayed, and even the order in which the objects were arranged suggested a tidying-up done that very morning. The gravel on the floor was neatly smoothed, and not a speck of dust was anywhere to be observed. Over the large outer coffin a pall of fine linen was laid, not rotting and falling to pieces like the cloth of mediæval times we see in our museums, but soft and strong like the sheets of our beds. In the clear space before the coffin stood a wooden pedestal in the form of a miniature lotus column. On the top of this, resting on three wooden prongs, was a small copper dish, in which were the ashes of incense, and the little stick used for stirring them. One asked oneself in bewilderment whether the ashes here, seemingly not cold, had truly ceased to glow at a time when Rome and Greece were undreamt of, when Assyria did not exist, and when the Exodus of the Children of Israel was yet unaccomplished.

On low tables round cakes of bread were laid out, not cracked and shrivelled, but smooth and brown, with a kind of white-of-egg glaze upon them. Onions and fruit were also spread out; and the fruit of the *dôm* palm was to be seen in plenty. In various parts of the chamber there were numerous bronze vessels of different shapes, intended for the holding of milk and other drinkables.

Well supplied with food and drink, the senses of the dead man were soothed by a profusion of flowers, which lay withered but not decayed beside the coffin, and which at the time of the funeral must have filled the chamber with their sweetness. Near the doorway stood an upright wooden chest closed with a lid. Opening this, we found it to contain the great ceremonial wig of the deceased man, which was suspended from a rail passing across the top of the chest, and hung free of the sides and bottom. The black hair was plaited into hundreds of little tails, but in size the wig was not unlike those of the early eighteenth century in Europe. Chairs, beds, and other pieces of furniture were arranged around the room, and at one side there were a number of small chests and boxes piled up against the wall. We opened one or two of these, and found them to contain delicate little vases of glass, stone, and metal, wrapped round with rags to prevent them breaking. These, like everything else in the tomb, were new and fresh, and showed no trace of the passing of the years.

The coffins, of course, were hidden by the great casing in which each rested, and which itself was partly hidden by the linen pall. Nothing could be touched for many days, until photographs had been taken and records made; and we therefore returned through the long passage to the light of the day.

There must have been a large number of intact tombs to be found when first the modern interest in Egyptian antiquities developed; but the market thus created had to be supplied, and gangs of illicit diggers made short work of the most accessible tombs. This illegal excavation, of course, continues to some extent at the present day, in spite of all precautions, but the results are becoming less and less proportionate to the labour expended and risk taken. A native likes best to do a little quiet digging in his own back yard and to admit nobody else into the business. To illustrate this, I may mention a tragedy which was brought to my notice a few years ago. A certain native discovered the entrance of a tomb in the floor of his stable, and at once proceeded to worm his way down the tunnel. That was the end of the native. His wife, finding that he had not returned two hours or so later, went down the newly found tunnel after him. That was the end of her also. In turn, three other members of the family went down into the darkness; and that was the end of them. A native official was then called, and, lighting his way with a candle, penetrated down the winding passage. The air was so foul that he was soon obliged to retreat, but he stated that he was just able to see in the distance ahead the bodies of the unfortunate peasants, all of whom had been overcome by what he quaintly described as "the evil lighting and bad climate." Various attempts at the rescue of the bodies having failed, we gave orders that this tomb should be regarded as their sepulchre, and that its mouth should be sealed up. According to the natives, there was evidently a vast hoard of wealth stored at the bottom of this tomb, and the would-be robbers had met their death at the hands of the demon in charge of it, who had seized each man by the throat as he came down the tunnel and had strangled him.

The Egyptian peasants have a very strong belief in the power of such creatures of the spirit world. A native who was attempting recently to discover hidden treasure in a certain part of the desert, sacrificed a lamb each night above the spot where he believed the treasure to lie, in order to propitiate the *djin* who guarded it. On the other hand, however, they have no superstition as regards the sanctity of the ancient dead, and they do not hesitate on that ground to rifle the tombs. Thousands of graves have been desecrated by these seekers after treasure, and it is very largely the result of this that scientific excavation is often so fruitless nowadays. When an excavator states that he has discovered a tomb, one takes it for granted that he means a *plundered* tomb, unless he definitely says that it was intact, in which case one calls him a lucky fellow and regards him with green envy.

And thus we come back to my remarks at the beginning of this chapter, that there is a painful disillusionment awaiting the man who comes to dig in Egypt in the hope of finding the golden cities of the Pharaohs or the bejewelled bodies of their dead. Of the latter there are but a few left to be found. The discovery of one of them forms the subject of the next chapter.

# CHAPTER VIII.

## THE TOMB OF TIY AND AKHNATON.[1]

In January 1907 the excavations in the Valley of the Tombs of the Kings at Thebes, which are being conducted each year by Mr Davis, brought to light the entrance of a tomb which, by its style, appeared to be that of a royal personage of the XVIIIth Dynasty. The Valley lies behind the cliffs which form the western boundary of Thebes, and is approached by a long winding road running between the rocks and rugged hills of the Lybian desert. Here the Pharaohs of the XVIIIth to the XXth Dynasties were buried in large sepulchres cut into the sides of the hills; and the present excavations have for their object the removal of the *débris* which has collected at the foot of these hills, in order that the tombs hidden beneath may be revealed. About sixty tombs are now open, some of which were already known to Greek and Roman travellers; and there are probably not more than two or three still to be discovered.

When this new tomb-entrance was uncovered I was at once notified, and proceeded with all despatch to the Valley. It was not long before we were able to enter the tomb. A rough stairway led down into the hillside, bringing us to the mouth of a passage which was entirely blocked by a wall of built stones. On removing this wall we found ourselves in a small passage, descending at a sharp incline to a chamber which could be seen a few yards farther on. Instead of this passage being free from *débris*,

---

1 A few paragraphs in this chapter also appear in my 'Life and Times of Akhnaton, Pharaoh of Egypt.' (Wm. Blackwood & Sons, 1910.)

however, as we had expected on finding the entrance-wall intact, it was partly filled with fallen stones which seemed to be the ruins of an earlier entrance-wall. On top of this heap of stones lay one of the sides of a large funeral shrine, almost entirely blocking the passage. This shrine, as we later saw, was in the form of a great box-like sarcophagus, made of cedar-wood covered with gold, and it had been intended as an outer covering for the coffin of the deceased person. It was, however, not put together: three sides of it were leaning against the walls of the burial-chamber, and the fourth was here in the passage. Either it was never built up, or else it was in process of being taken out of the tomb again when the work was abandoned.

PL. XVIII. The entrance of the tomb of Queen Tiy, with Egyptian policeman standing beside it. On the left is the later tomb of Rameses X.

*[Photo by R. Paul.]*

To pass this portion of the shrine which lay in the passage without doing it damage was no easy matter. We could not venture to move it, as the wood was rotten; and indeed, for over a year it remained in its original position. We therefore made a bridge of planks within a few inches of the low roof, and on this we wriggled ourselves across into the unencumbered passage beyond. In the funeral-chamber, besides the other portions of the shrine, we found at one corner a splendid coffin, in the usual form of a recumbent figure, inlaid in a dazzling manner with rare stones and coloured glass. The coffin had originally lain upon a wooden bier, in the form of a lion-legged couch; but this had collapsed and the mummy had fallen to the ground, the lid of the coffin being partly thrown off by the fall, thus exposing the head and feet of the body, from which the bandages had decayed and fallen off. In the powerful glare of the electric light which we carried, the bare skull, with a golden vulture upon it, could be seen protruding from the remains of the linen bandages and from the sheets of flexible gold-foil in which, as we afterwards found, the whole body was wrapped. The inscription on the coffin, the letters of which were made of rare stones, gave the titles of Akhnaton, "the beautiful child of the Sun"; but turning to the shrine we found other inscriptions stating that King Akhnaton had made it for his mother, Queen Tiy, and thus no immediate reply could be given to those at the mouth of the tomb who called to us to know which of the Pharaoh's of Egypt had been found.

In a recess in the wall above the body there stood four alabaster "canopy" jars, each with a lid exquisitely sculptured in the form of a human head. In another corner there was a box containing many little toilet vases and utensils of porcelain. A few alabaster vases and other objects were lying in various parts of the chamber, arranged in some sort of rough order.

Nothing, of course, could yet be touched, and for several days, during the lengthy process of photographing and recording the contents of the tomb *in situ*, no further information could be obtained as to the identity of the owner of the tomb. The shrine was certainly made for Queen Tiy, and so too were the toilet utensils, judging by an inscription upon one of them which gave the names of Tiy and her husband, King Amenhotep III., the parents of Akhnaton. It was, therefore, not a surprise when a passing doctor declared the much broken bones to be those of a woman—that is to say, those of Queen Tiy. For reasons which will presently become apparent, it had been difficult to believe that Akhnaton could have been buried in this Valley, and one was very ready to suppose that the coffin bearing his name had but been given by him to his mother.

The important discovery was now announced, and considerable interest and excitement. At the end of the winter the various archæologists departed to their several countries, and it fell to me to despatch the antiquities to the Cairo Museum, and to send the bones, soaked in wax to prevent their breakage, to Dr Elliot Smith, to be examined by that eminent authority. It may be imagined that my surprise was considerable when I received a letter from him reading—"Are you sure that the bones you sent me are those which were found in the tomb? Instead of the bones of an old woman, you have sent me those of a young man. Surely there is some mistake."

There was, however, no mistake. Dr Elliot Smith later informed me that the bones were those of a young man of about twenty-eight years of age, and at first this description did not seem to tally with that of Akhnaton, who was always thought to have been a man of middle age. But there is now no possibility of doubt that the coffin and mummy were those of this extraordinary Pharaoh, although the tomb and funeral furniture belonged to Queen Tiy. Dr Elliot Smith's decision was, of course, somewhat disconcerting to those who had written of the mortal remains of the great Queen; but it is difficult to speak of Tiy without also referring to her famous son Akhnaton, and in these articles he had received full mention.

About the year B.C. 1500 the throne of Egypt fell to the young brother of Queen Hatshepsut, Thutmosis III., and under his vigorous rule the country rose to a height of power never again equalled. Amenhotep II. succeeded to an empire which extended from the Sudan to the Euphrates and to the Greek Islands; and when he died he left these great possessions almost intact to his son, Thutmosis IV., the grandfather of Akhnaton. It is important to notice the chronology of this period. The mummy of Thutmosis IV. has been shown by Dr Elliot Smith to be that of a man of not more than twenty-six years of age; but we know that his son Amenhotep III. was old enough to hunt lions at about the time of his father's death, and that he was already married to Queen Tiy a year later. Thus one must suppose that Thutmosis IV. was a father at the age of thirteen or fourteen, and that Amenhotep III. was married to Tiy at about the same age. The wife of Thutmosis IV. was probably a Syrian princess, and it must have been during her regency that Amenhotep III. married Tiy, who was not of royal blood. Amenhotep and Tiy introduced into Egypt the luxuries of Asia; and during their brilliant reign the Nile Valley was more open to Syrian influence than it had ever been before. The language of Babylon was perhaps the Court tongue, and the correspondence was written in cuneiform instead of in the hieratic script of Egypt. Amenhotep III., as has been said, was probably partly Asiatic; and there is, perhaps, some reason to suppose that Yuaa, the father of Queen Tiy, was also a Syrian. One has, therefore, to picture the Egyptian Court at this time as being saturated with foreign ideas, which clashed with those of the orthodox Egyptians.

Queen Tiy bore several children to the King; but it was not until they had reigned over twenty years that a son and heir was born, whom they named Amenhotep, that being changed later to Akhnaton. It is probable that he first saw the light in the royal palace at Thebes, which was situated on the edge of the desert at the foot of the western hills. It was an extensive and roomy structure, lightly built and gaily decorated. The ceiling and pavements of its halls were fantastically painted with scenes of animal life: wild cattle ran through reedy swamps beneath one's feet, and many-coloured fish swam in the water; while overhead flights of pigeons, white against a blue sky, passed across the hall, and the wild duck hastened towards the open casements. Through curtained doorways one might obtain glimpses of a garden planted with flowers foreign to Egypt; and on the east of the palace the King had made a great pleasure-lake for the Queen, surrounded by the trees of Asia. Here, floating in her golden barge, which was named *Aton-gleams*, the Queen might look westwards over the tree-tops to the splendid Theban hills towering above the palace, and eastwards to the green valley of the Nile and the three great limestone hills beyond. Amenhotep III. has been rightly called the "Magnificent," and one may well believe that his son Akhnaton was born to the sound of music and to the clink of golden wine-cups. Fragments of countless thousands of wine-jars and blue fayence drinking-vessels have been found in the ruins of the palace; and contemporary objects and paintings show us some of the exquisitely wrought bowls of gold and silver which must have graced the royal tables, and the charming toilet utensils which were to be found in the sleeping apartments.

While the luxurious Court rejoiced at the birth of this Egypto-Asiatic prince, one feels that the ancient priesthood of Amon-Ra must have stood aloof, and must have looked askance at the baby who was destined one day to be their master. This priesthood was perhaps the proudest and most conservative community which conservative Egypt ever produced. It demanded implicit obedience to its stiff and ancient conventions, and it refused to recognise the growing tendency towards religious speculation. One of the great gods of Syria was Aton, the god of the sun; and his recognition at the Theban Court was a source of constant irritation to the ministers of Amon-Ra.

PL. XIX. Toilet-spoons of carved wood, discovered in tombs of the Eighteenth Dynasty. That on the right has a movable lid.—CAIRO MUSEUM.
*[Photo by E. Brugsch Pasha.]*

Probably they would have taken stronger measures to resist this foreign god had it not been for the fact that Atum of Heliopolis, an ancient god of Egypt, was on the one hand closely akin to Ra, the associated deity with Amon, and on the other hand to Aton of Syria. Thus Aton might be regarded merely as another name for Ra or Amon-Ra; but the danger to the old *régime* lay in the fact that with the worship of Aton there went a certain amount of freethought. The sun and its warm rays were the heritage of all mankind; and the speculative mind of the Asiatic, always in advance of the less imaginative Egyptian, had not failed to collect to the Aton-worship a number of semi-philosophical teachings far broader than the strict doctrines of Amon-Ra could tolerate.

There is much reason to suppose that Queen Tiy was the prime factor in the new movement. It may, perhaps, be worth noting that her father was a priest of the Egyptian god Min, who corresponded to the North Syrian Aton in his capacity as a god of vegetation; and she may have imbibed something of the broader doctrines from him. It is the barge upon *her* pleasure-lake which is called *Aton-gleams*, and it is *her* private artist who is responsible for one of the first examples of the new style of art which begins to appear at this period. Egyptian art was bound down by conventions jealously guarded by the priesthood, and the slight tendency to break away from these, which now becomes apparent, is another sign of the broadening of thought under the reign of Amenhotep III. and Tiy.

King Amenhotep III. does not seem to have been a man of strong character, and in the changes which took place at this time he does not appear to have taken so very large a part. He always showed the most profound respect for, and devotion to, his Queen; and one is inclined to regard him as a tool in her hands. According to some accounts he reigned only thirty years, but there are contemporary monuments dated in his thirty-sixth year, and it seems probable that for the last few years he was reigning only in name, and that in reality his ministers, under the regency of Queen Tiy, governed the land. Amenhotep III. was perhaps during his last years insane or stricken with some paralytic disease, for we read of an Asiatic monarch sending a miracle-working image to Egypt, apparently for the purpose of attempting to cure him. It must have been during these six years of absolute power, while Akhnaton was a boy, that the Queen pushed forward her reforms and encouraged the breaking down of the old traditions, especially those relating to the worship of Amon-Ra.

Amenhotep III. died in about the forty-ninth year of his age, after a total reign of thirty-six years; and Akhnaton, who still bore the name of Amenhotep, ascended the throne. One must picture him now as an enthusiastic boy, filled with the new thought of the age, and burning to assert the broad doctrines which he had learned from his mother and her friends, in defiance of the priests of Amon-Ra. He was already married to a Syrian named Nefertiti, and certainly before he was fifteen years of age he was the father of two daughters.

The new Pharaoh's first move, under the guidance of Tiy, was to proclaim Aton the only true god, and to name himself high priest of that deity. He then began to build a temple dedicated to Aton at Karnak; but it must have been distasteful to observe how overshadowed and dwarfed was this new temple by the mighty buildings in honour of the older gods which stood there. Moreover, there must have been very serious opposition to the new religion in Thebes, where Amon had ruled for so many centuries unchallenged. In whatever direction he looked he was confronted with some evidence of the worship of Amon-Ra: he might proclaim Aton to be the only god, but Amon and a hundred other deities stared down at him from every temple wall. He and his advisers, therefore, decided to abandon Thebes altogether and to found a new capital elsewhere.

Akhnaton selected a site for the new city on the west bank of the river, at a point now named El Amarna, about 160 miles above Cairo. Here the hills recede from the river, forming a bay about three miles deep and five long; and in this bay the young Pharaoh decided to build his capital, which was named "Horizon of Aton." With feverish speed the new buildings were erected. A palace even more beautiful than that of his parents at Thebes was prepared for him; a splendid temple dedicated to Aton was set up amidst a garden of rare trees and brilliant flowers; villas for his nobles were erected, and streets were laid out. Queen Tiy, who seems to have continued to live at Thebes, often came down to El Amarna to visit her son; but it seems to have been at his own wish rather than at her advice that he now took the important step which set the seal of his religion upon his life.

Around the bay of El Amarna, on the cliffs which shut it off so securely, the King caused landmarks to be made at intervals, and on these he inscribed an oath which some have interpreted to mean that he would never again leave his new city. He would remain, like the Pope in the Vatican, for the rest of his days within the limits of this bay; and, rather than be distracted by the cares of state and the worries of empire, he would shut himself up with his god and would devote his life to his religion. He was but a youth still, and, to his inexperienced mind, this oath seemed nothing; nor in his brief life does it seem that he broke it, though at times he must have longed to visit his domains.

The religion which this boy, who now called himself Akhnaton, "The Glory of Aton," taught was by no means the simple worship of the sun. It was, without question, the most enlightened religion which the world at that time had ever known. The young priest-king called upon mankind to worship the unknown power which is behind the sun, that power of which the brilliant sun was the visible symbol, and which might be discerned in the fertilising warmth of the sun's rays. Aton was originally the actual sun's disk; but Akhnaton called his god "Heat which is in Aton," and thus drew the eyes of his followers towards a Force far more intangible and distant than the dazzling orb to which they bowed down. Akhnaton's god was the force which created the sun, the something which penetrated to this earth in the sun's heat and caused the vegetation to grow.

Amon-Ra and the gods of Egypt were for the most part but deified mortals, endued with monstrous, though limited, power, and still having around them traditions of exaggerated human deeds. Others had their origin in natural phenomena—the wind, the Nile, the sky, and so on. All were terrific, revengeful, and able to be moved by human emotions. But Akhnaton's god was the intangible and yet ever-present Father of mankind, made manifest in sunshine. The youthful High Priest called upon his followers to search for their god not in the confusion of battle or behind the smoke of human sacrifices, but amidst the flowers and trees, amidst the wild duck and the fishes. He preached an enlightened nature-study; he was perhaps the first apostle of the Simple Life. He strove to break down conventional religion, and ceaselessly urged his people to worship in Truth, simply, without an excess of ceremonial. While the elder gods had been manifest in natural convulsions and in the more awful incidents of life, Akhnaton's kindly god could be seen in the chick which broke out of its egg, in the wind which filled the sails of the ships, in the fish which leapt from the water. Aton was the joy which caused the young sheep "to dance upon their feet," and the birds to "flutter in their marshes." He was the god of the simple pleasures of life, and Truth was the watchword of his followers.

It may be understood how the boy longed for truth in all things when one remembers the thousand exaggerated conventions of Egyptian life at this time. Court etiquette had developed to a degree which rendered life to the Pharaoh an endless round of unnatural poses of mind and body. In the preaching of his doctrine of truth and simplicity, Akhnaton did not fail to call upon his subjects to regard their Pharaoh not as a god but as a man. It was usual for the Pharaoh to keep aloof from his people: Akhnaton was to be found in their midst. The Court demanded that their lord should drive in solitary state through the city: Akhnaton sat in his chariot with his wife and children, and allowed the artist to represent him joking with his little daughter, who has mischievously poked the horses with a stick. In representing the Pharaoh, the artist was expected to draw him in some conventional attitude of dignity: Akhnaton insisted upon being shown in all manner of natural attitudes—now leaning languidly upon a staff, now nursing his children, now caressing his wife.

As has been said, one of the first artists to break away from the ancient conventions was in the service of Queen Tiy, and was probably under her influence. But in the radical change in the art which took place, Akhnaton is definitely stated to have been the leader, and the new school acknowledge that they were taught by the King. The new art is extraordinary, and it must be owned that its merit lies rather in its originality than in its beauty. An attempt is made to do away with the prescribed attitudes and the strict proportions, and to portray any one individual with his natural defects. Some of the sculptured heads, however, which have come down to us, and notably the four "canopic" heads found in this tomb, are of wonderful beauty, and have no trace of traditional mannerisms, though they are highly idealised. The King's desire for light-heartedness led him to encourage the use of bright colours and gay decorations in the palace. Some of the ceiling and pavement paintings are of great beauty, while the walls and pillars inlaid with coloured stones must have given a brilliancy to the halls unequalled in Egypt at any previous time.

The group of nobles who formed the King's Court had all sacrificed much in coming to the new capital. Their estates around Thebes had been left, their houses abandoned, and the tombs which were in process of being made for them in the Theban hills had been rendered useless. The King, therefore, showered favours upon them, and at his expense built their houses and constructed sepulchres for them. It is on the walls of these tombs that one obtains the main portion of one's information regarding the teachings of this wonderful youth, who was now growing into manhood. Here are inscribed those beautiful hymns to Aton which rank so high in ancient literature. It is unfortunate that space does not allow more than a few extracts from the hymns to be quoted here; but something of their beauty may be realised from these. (Professor Breasted's translation.)

"Thy dawning is beautiful in the horizon of heaven,
O living Aton, Beginning of life!
When thou risest in the eastern horizon of heaven
Thou fillest every land with thy beauty."

"Though thou art afar, thy rays are on earth;
Though thou art on high, thy footprints are the day."

"When thou settest in the western horizon of heaven
The world is in darkness like the dead.
Men sleep in their chambers, their heads are wrapt up.
Every lion cometh forth from his den.
The serpents, they sting.
Darkness reigns, the world is in silence:
He that made them has gone to rest in his horizon."

"Bright is the earth when thou risest in the horizon . . .
When thou sendest forth thy rays
The two lands of Egypt are in daily festivity,
Awake and standing upon their feet,
For thou hast raised them up.
Their limbs bathed, they take their clothing,
Their arms uplifted in adoration to thy dawning.
Then in all the world they do their work."

"All cattle rest upon their herbage, all trees and plants flourish.
The birds flutter in their marshes, their wings uplifted in adoration to thee.
All the sheep dance upon their feet,
All winged things fly; they live when thou hast shone upon them."

"The barques sail up-stream and down-stream alike, . . .
The fish in the river leap up before thee,
And thy rays are in the midst of the great sea."

"Thou art he who createst the man-child in woman . . .
Who giveth life to the son in the body of his mother;
Who soothest him that he may not weep,
A nurse even in the womb."

"When the chick crieth in the egg-shell,
Thou givest him breath therein to preserve him alive . . .
He cometh forth from the egg, to chirp with all his might.
He runneth about upon his two feet."

"How manifold are all thy works!
They are hidden from before us."

There are several verses of this hymn which are almost identical with Psalm civ., and those who study it closely will be forced to one of two conclusions: either that Psalm civ. is derived from this hymn of the young Pharaoh, or that both are derived from some early Syrian hymn to the sun. Akhnaton may have only adapted this early psalm to local conditions; though, on the other hand, a man capable of bringing to pass so great a religious revolution in Egypt may well be credited with the authorship of this splendid song. There is no evidence to show that it was written before the King had reached manhood.

Queen Tiy probably did not now take any further part in a movement which had got so far out of her hands. She was now nearly sixty years old, and this, to one who had been a mother so early in life, was a considerable age. It seems that she sometimes paid visits to her son at El Amarna, but her interest lay in Thebes, where she had once held so brilliant a Court. When at last she died, therefore, it is not surprising to find that she was buried in the Valley of the Tombs of the Kings. The tomb which has been described above is most probably her original sepulchre, and here her body was placed in the golden shrine made for her by Akhnaton, surrounded by the usual funeral furniture. She thus lay no more than a stone's throw from her parents, whose tomb was discovered two years ago, and which was of very similar size and shape.

After her death, although preaching this gentle creed of love and simple truth, Akhnaton waged a bitter and stern war against the priesthoods of the old gods. It may be that the priesthoods of Amon had again attempted to overthrow the new doctrines, or had in some manner called down the particular wrath of the Pharaoh. He issued an order that the name of Amon was to be erased and obliterated wherever it was found, and his agents proceeded to hack it out on all the temple walls. The names also of other gods were erased; and it is noticeable in this tomb that the word *mut*, meaning "mother," was carefully spelt in hieroglyphs which would have no similarity to those used in the word *Mut*, the goddess-consort of Amon. The name of Amenhotep III., his own father, did not escape the King's wrath, and the first syllables were everywhere erased.

As the years went by Akhnaton seems to have given himself more and more completely to his new religion. He had now so trained one of his nobles, named Merira, in the teachings of Aton that he was able to hand over to him the high priesthood of that god, and to turn his attention to the many other duties which he had imposed upon himself. In rewarding Merira, the King is related to have said, "Hang gold at his neck before and behind, and gold on his legs, because of his hearing the teaching of Pharaoh concerning every saying in these beautiful places." Another official whom Akhnaton greatly advanced says: "My lord advanced me because I have carried out his teaching, and I hear his word without ceasing." The King's doctrines were thus beginning to take hold; but one feels, nevertheless, that the nobles followed their King rather for the sake of their material gains than for the spiritual comforts of the Aton-worship. There is reason to suppose that at least one of these nobles was degraded and banished from the city.

But while Akhnaton was preaching peace and goodwill amidst the flowers of the temple of Aton, his generals in Asia Minor were vainly struggling to hold together the great empire created by Thutmosis III. Akhnaton had caused a temple of Aton to be erected at one point in Syria at least, but in other respects he took little or no interest in the welfare of his foreign dominions. War was not tolerated in his doctrine: it was a sin to take away life which the good Father had given. One pictures the hardened soldiers of the empire striving desperately to hold the nations of Asia faithful to the Pharaoh whom they never saw. The small garrisons were scattered far and wide over Syria, and constantly they sent messengers to the Pharaoh asking at least for some sign that he held them in mind.

There is no more pathetic page of ancient history than that which tells of the fall of the Egyptian Empire. The Amorites, advancing along the sea-coast, took city after city from the Egyptians almost without a struggle. The chiefs of Tunip wrote an appeal for help to the King: "To the King of Egypt, my lord,—The inhabitants of Tunip, thy servant." The plight of the city is described and reinforcements are asked for, "And now," it continues, "Tunip thy city weeps, and her tears are flowing, and there is no help for us. For twenty years we have been sending to our lord the King, the King of Egypt, but there has not come a word to us, no, not one." The messengers of the beleaguered city must have found the King absorbed in his religion, and must have seen only priests of the sun where they had hoped to find the soldiers of former days. The Egyptian governor of Jerusalem, attacked by Aramæans, writes to the Pharaoh, saying: "Let the King take care of his land, and . . . let send troops . . . For if no troops come in this year, the whole territory of my lord the King will perish." To this letter is added a note to the King's secretary, which reads, "Bring these words plainly before my lord the King: the whole land of my lord the King is going to ruin."

So city after city fell, and the empire, won at such cost, was gradually lost to the Egyptians. It is probable that Akhnaton had not realised how serious was the situation in Asia Minor. A few of the chieftains who were not actually in arms against him had written to him every now and then assuring him that all was well in his dominions; and, strange to relate, the tribute of many of the cities had been regularly paid. The Asiatic princes, in fact, had completely fooled the Pharaoh, and had led him to believe that the nations were loyal while they themselves prepared for rebellion. Akhnaton, hating violence, had been only too ready to believe that the despatches from Tunip and elsewhere were unjustifiably pessimistic. He had hoped to bind together the many countries under his rule, by giving them a single religion. He had hoped that when Aton should be worshipped in all parts of his empire, and when his simple doctrines of love, truth, and peace should be preached from every temple throughout the length and breadth of his dominions, then war would cease and a unity of faith would hold the lands in harmony one with the other.

When, therefore, the tribute suddenly ceased, and the few refugees came staggering home to tell of the perfidy of the Asiatic princes and the fall of the empire, Akhnaton seems to have received his deathblow. He was now not more than twenty-eight years of age; and though his portraits show that his face was already lined with care, and that his body was thinner than it should have been, he seems to have had plenty of reserve strength. He was the father of several daughters, but his queen had borne him no son to succeed him; and thus he must have felt that his religion could not outlive him. With his empire lost, with Thebes his enemy, and with his treasury wellnigh empty, one feels that Akhnaton must have sunk to the very depths of despondency. His religious revolution had ruined Egypt, and had failed: did he, one wonders, find consolation in the sunshine and amidst the flowers?

His death followed speedily; and, resting in the splendid coffin in which we found him, he was laid in the tomb prepared for him in the hills behind his new capital. The throne fell to the husband of one of his daughters, Smenkhkara, who, after an ephemeral reign, gave place to another of the sons-in-law of Akhnaton, Tutankhaton. This king was speedily persuaded to change his name to Tutankhamon, to abandon the worship of Aton, and to return to Thebes. Akhnaton's city fell into ruins, and soon the temples and palaces became the haunt of jackals and the home of owls. The nobles returned with their new king to Thebes, and not one remained faithful to those "teachings" to which they had once pretended to be such earnest listeners.

PL. XX. The coffin of Akhnaton lying in the tomb of Queen Tiy.
*[Photo by R. Paul.]*

The fact that the body in the new tomb was that of Akhnaton, and not of Queen Tiy, gives a new reading to the history of the burial. When

Tutankhamon returned to Thebes, Akhnaton's memory was still, it appears, regarded with reverence, and it seems that there was no question of leaving his body in the neighbourhood of his deserted palace, where, until the discovery of this tomb, Egyptologists had expected to find it. It was carried to Thebes, together with some of the funeral furniture, and was placed in the tomb of Queen Tiy, which had been reopened for the purpose. But after some years had passed and the priesthood of Amon-Ra had again asserted itself, Akhnaton began to be regarded as a heretic and as the cause of the loss of Egypt's Asiatic dominions. These sentiments were vigorously encouraged by the priesthood, and soon Akhnaton came to be spoken of as "that criminal," and his name was obliterated from his monuments. It was now felt that his body could no longer lie in state together with that of Queen Tiy in the Valley of the Tombs of the Kings. The sepulchre was therefore opened once more, and the name Akhnaton was everywhere erased from the inscriptions. The tomb, polluted by the presence of the heretic, was no longer fit for Tiy, and the body of the Queen was therefore carried elsewhere, perhaps to the tomb of her husband Amenhotep III. The shrine in which her mummy had lain was pulled to pieces and an attempt was made to carry it out of the tomb; but this arduous task was presently abandoned, and one portion of the shrine was left in the passage, where we found it. The body of Akhnaton, his name erased, was now the sole occupant of the tomb. The entrance was blocked with stones, and sealed with the seal of Tutankhamon, a fragment of which was found; and it was in this condition that it was discovered in 1907.

The bones of this extraordinary Pharaoh are in the Cairo Museum; but, in deference to the sentiments of many worthy persons, they are not exhibited. The visitor to that museum, however, may now see the "canopic" jars, the alabaster vases, the gold vulture, the gold necklace, the sheets of gold in which the body was wrapped, the toilet utensils, and parts of the shrine, all of which we found in the burial-chamber.

# CHAPTER IX.

## THE TOMB OF HOREMHEB.

In the last chapter a discovery was recorded which, as experience has shown, is of considerable interest to the general reader. The romance and the tragedy of the life of Akhnaton form a really valuable addition to the store of good things which is our possession, and which the archæologist so diligently labours to increase. Curiously enough, another discovery, that of the tomb of Horemheb, was made by the same explorer (Mr Davis) in 1908; and as it forms the natural sequel to the previous chapter, I may be permitted to record it here.

Akhnaton was succeeded by Smenkhkara, his son-in-law, who, after a brief reign, gave place to Tutankhamon, during whose short life the court returned to Thebes. A certain noble named Ay came next to the throne, but held it for only three years. The country was now in a chaotic condition, and was utterly upset and disorganised by the revolution of Akhnaton, and by the vacillating policy of the three weak kings who succeeded him, each reigning for so short a time. One cannot say to what depths of degradation Egypt might have sunk had it not been for the timely appearance of Horemheb, a wise and good ruler, who, though but a soldier of not particularly exalted birth, managed to raise himself to the vacant throne, and succeeded in so organising the country once more that his successors, Rameses I., Sety I., and Rameses II., were able to regain most of the lost dominions, and to place Egypt at the head of the nations of the world.

Horemheb, "The Hawk in Festival," was born at Alabastronpolis, a city of the 18th Province of Upper Egypt, during the reign of Amenhotep III., who has rightly been named "The Magnificent," and in whose reign Egypt was at once the most powerful, the most wealthy, and the most luxurious country in the world. There is reason to suppose that Horemheb's family were of noble birth, and it is thought by some that an inscription which calls King Thutmosis III. "the father of his fathers" is to be taken literally to mean that that old warrior was his great-or great-great-grandfather. The young noble was probably educated at the splendid court of Amenhotep III., where the wit and intellect of the world was congregated, and where, under the presidency of the beautiful Queen Tiy, life slipped by in a round of revels.

As an impressionable young man, Horemheb must have watched the gradual development of freethought in the palace, and the ever-increasing irritation and chafing against the bonds of religious convention which bound all Thebans to the worship of the god Amon. Judging by his future actions, Horemheb did not himself feel any real repulsion to Amon, though the religious rut into which the country had fallen was sufficiently objectionable to a man of his intellect to cause him to cast in his lot with the movement towards emancipation. In later life he would certainly have been against the movement, for his mature judgment led him always to be on the side of ordered habit and custom as being less dangerous to the national welfare than a social upheaval or change.

Horemheb seems now to have held the appointment of captain or commander in the army, and at the same time, as a "Royal Scribe," he cultivated the art of letters, and perhaps made himself acquainted with those legal matters which in later years he was destined to reform.

When Amenhotep III. died, the new king, Akhnaton, carried out the revolution which had been pending for many years, and absolutely banned the worship of Amon, with all that it involved. He built himself a new capital at El Amârna, and there he instituted the worship of the sun, or rather of the heat or power of the sun, under the name of Aton. In so far as the revolution constituted a breaking away from tiresome convention, the young Horemheb seems to have been with the King. No one of intelligence could deny that the new religion and new philosophy which was preached at El Amârna was more worthy of consideration on general lines than was the narrow doctrine of the Amon priesthood; and all thinkers must have rejoiced at the freedom from bonds which had become intolerable. But the world was not ready, and indeed is still not ready, for the schemes which Akhnaton propounded; and the unpractical model-kingdom which was uncertainly developing under the hills of El Amârna must have already been seen to contain the elements of grave danger to the State.

Nevertheless the revolution offered many attractions. The frivolous members of the court, always ready for change and excitement, welcomed with enthusiasm the doctrine of the moral and simple life which the King and his advisers preached, just as in the decadent days before the French Revolution the court, bored with licentiousness, gaily welcomed the morality-painting of the young Greuze. And to the more serious-minded, such as Horemheb seems to have been, the movement must have appealed in its imperial aspect. The new god Aton was largely worshipped in Syria, and it seems evident that Akhnaton had hoped to bind together the heterogeneous nations of the empire by a bond of common worship. The Asiatics were not disposed to worship Amon, but Aton appealed to them as much as any god, and Horemheb must have seen great possibilities in a common religion.

It is thought that Horemheb may be identified amongst the nobles who followed Akhnaton to El Amârna, and though this is not certain, there is little doubt that he was in high favour with the King at the time. To one whose tendency is neither towards frivolity nor towards fanaticism, there can be nothing more broadening than the influence of religious changes. More than one point of view is appreciated: a man learns that there are other ruts than that in which he runs, and so he seeks the smooth midway. Thus Horemheb, while acting loyally towards his King, and while appreciating the value of the new movement, did not exclude from his thoughts those teachings which he deemed good in the old order of things. He seems to have seen life broadly; and when the new religion of Akhnaton became narrowed and fanatical, as it did towards the close of the tragic chapter of that king's short life, Horemheb was one of the few men who kept an open mind.

Like many other nobles of the period, he had constructed for himself a tomb at Sakkâra, in the shadow of the pyramids of the old kings of Egypt; and fragments of this tomb, which of course was abandoned when he became Pharaoh, are now to be seen in various museums. In one of the scenes there sculptured Horemheb is shown in the presence of a king who is almost certainly Akhnaton; and yet in a speech to him inscribed above the reliefs, Horemheb makes reference to the god Amon whose very name was anathema to the King. The royal figure is drawn according to the canons of art prescribed by Akhnaton, and upon which, as a protest against the conventional art of the old order, he laid the greatest stress in his revolution; and thus, at all events, Horemheb was in sympathy with this aspect of the movement. But the inscriptions which refer to Amon, and yet are impregnated with the Aton style of expression, show that Horemheb was not to be held down to any one mode of thought. Akhnaton was, perhaps, already dead when these inscriptions were added, and thus

Horemheb may have had no further reason to hide his views; or it may be that they constituted a protest against that narrowness which marred the last years of a pious king.

Those who read the history of the period in the last chapter will remember how Akhnaton came to persecute the worshippers of Amon, and how he erased that god's name wherever it was written throughout the length and breadth of Egypt. Evidently with this action Horemheb did not agree; nor was this his only cause for complaint. As an officer, and now a highly placed general of the army, he must have seen with feelings of the utmost bitterness the neglected condition of the Syrian provinces. Revolt after revolt occurred in these states; but Akhnaton, dreaming and praying in the sunshine of El Amârna, would send no expedition to punish the rebels. Good-fellowship with all men was the King's watchword, and a policy more or less democratic did not permit him to make war on his fellow-creatures. Horemheb could smell battle in the distance, but could not taste of it. The battalions which he had trained were kept useless in Egypt; and even when, during the last years of Akhnaton's reign, or under his successor Smenkhkara, he was made commander-in-chief of all the forces, there was no means of using his power to check the loss of the cities of Asia. Horemheb must have watched these cities fall one by one into the hands of those who preached the doctrine of the sword, and there can be little wonder that he turned in disgust from the doings at El Amârna.

During the times which followed, when Smenkhkara held the throne for a year or so, and afterwards, when Tutankhamon became Pharaoh, Horemheb seems to have been the leader of the reactionary movement. He did not concern himself so much with the religious aspect of the questions: there was as much to be said on behalf of Aton as there was on behalf of Amon. But it was he who knocked at the doors of the heart of Egypt, and urged the nation to awake to the danger in the

East. An expedition against the rebels was organised, and one reads that Horemheb was the "companion of his Lord upon the battlefield on that day of the slaying of the Asiatics." Akhnaton had been opposed to warfare, and had dreamed that dream of universal peace which still is a far-off light to mankind. Horemheb was a practical man in whom such a dream would have been but weakness; and, though one knows nothing more of these early campaigns, the fact that he attempted to chastise the enemies of the empire at this juncture stands to his credit for all time.

Under Tutankhamon the court returned to Thebes, though not yet exclusively to the worship of Amon; and the political phase of the revolution came to an end. The country once more settled into the old order of life, and Horemheb, having experienced the full dangers of philosophic speculation, was glad enough to abandon thought for action. He was now the most powerful man in the kingdom, and inscriptions call him "the greatest of the great, the mightiest of the mighty, presider over the Two Lands of Egypt, general of generals," and so on. The King "appointed him to be Chief of the Land, to administer the laws of the land as Hereditary Prince of all this land"; and "all that was done was done by his command." From chaos Horemheb was producing order, and all men turned to him in gratitude as he reorganised the various government departments.

The offices which he held, such as Privy Councillor, King's Secretary, Great Lord of the People, and so on, are very numerous; and in all of these he dealt justly though sternly, so that "when he came the fear of him was great in the sight of the people, prosperity and health were craved for him, and he was greeted as 'Father of the Two Lands of Egypt.'" He was indeed the saviour and father of his country, for he had found her corrupt and disordered, and he was leading her back to greatness and dignity.

PL. XXI. Head of a granite statue of the god Khonsu, probably dating from about the period of Horemheb.
—CAIRO MUSEUM.
*[Photo by Beato.]*

At this time he was probably a man of about forty years of age. In appearance he seems to have been noble and good to look upon. "When he was born," says the inscription, "he was clothed with strength: the hue of a god was upon him"; and in later life, "the form of a god was in his colour," whatever that may mean. He was a man of considerable eloquence and great learning. "He astonished the people by that which came out of his mouth," we are told; and "when he was summoned before the King the palace began to fear." One may picture the weak Pharaoh and his corrupt court, as they watched with apprehension the movements of this stern soldier, of whom it was said that his every thought was "in the footsteps of the Ibis,"—the ibis being the god of wisdom.

On the death of Tutankhamon, the question of inviting Horemheb to fill the vacant throne must have been seriously considered; but there was another candidate, a certain Ay, who had been one of the most important nobles in the group of Akhnaton's favourites at El Amârna, and who had been the loudest in the praises of Aton. Religious feeling was at the time running high, for the partizans of Amon and those of Aton seem to have been waging war on one another; and Ay appears to have been regarded as the man most likely to bridge the gulf between the two parties. A favourite of Akhnaton, and once a devout worshipper of Aton, he was not averse to the cults of other gods; and by conciliating both factions he managed to obtain the throne for himself. His power, however, did not last for long; and as the priests of Amon regained the confidence of the nation at the expense of those of Aton, so the power of Ay declined. His past connections with Akhnaton told against him, and after a year or so he disappeared, leaving the throne vacant once more.

There was now no question as to who should succeed. A princess named Mutnezem, the sister of Akhnaton's queen, and probably an old friend of Horemheb, was the sole heiress to the throne, the last surviving member of the greatest Egyptian dynasty. All men turned to Horemheb in the hope that he would marry this lady, and thus reign as Pharaoh over them, perhaps leaving a son by her to succeed him when he was gathered to his fathers. He was now some forty-five years of age, full of energy and vigour, and passionately anxious to have a free hand in the carrying out of his schemes for the reorganisation of the government. It was therefore with joy that, in about the year 1350 B.C., he sailed up to Thebes in order to claim the crown.

He arrived at Luxor at a time when the annual festival of Amon was being celebrated, and all the city was *en fête*. The statue of the god had been taken from its shrine at Karnak, and had been towed up the river to Luxor in a gorgeous barge, attended by a fleet of gaily-decorated vessels. With songs and dancing it had been conveyed into the Luxor temple, where the priests had received it standing amidst piled-up masses of flowers, fruit, and other offerings. It seems to have been at this moment that Horemheb appeared, while the clouds of incense streamed up to heaven, and the morning air was full of the sound of the harps and the lutes. Surrounded by a crowd of his admirers, he was conveyed into the presence of the divine figure, and was there and then hailed as Pharaoh.

From the temple he was carried amidst cheering throngs to the palace which stood near by; and there he was greeted by the Princess Mutnezem, who fell on her knees before him and embraced him. That very day, it would seem, he was married to her, and in the evening the royal heralds published the style and titles by which he would be known in the future: "Mighty Bull, Ready in Plans; Favourite of the Two Goddesses, Great in Marvels; Golden Hawk, Satisfied with Truth; Creator of the Two Lands," and so forth. Then, crowned with the royal helmet, he was led once more before the statue of Amon, while the priests pronounced the blessing of the gods upon him. Passing down to the quay before the temple the figure of the god was placed once more upon the state-barge, and was floated down to Karnak; while Horemheb was led through the rejoicing crowds back to the palace to begin his reign as Pharaoh.

In religious matters Horemheb at once adopted a strong attitude of friendship towards the Amon party which represented the old order of things. There is evidence to show that Aton was in no way persecuted; yet one by one his shrines were abandoned, and the neglected temples of Amon and the elder gods once more rang with the hymns of praise. Inscriptions tell us that the King "restored the temples from the marshes of the Delta to Nubia. He fashioned a hundred images with all their bodies correct, and with all splendid costly stones. He established for them daily offerings every day. All the vessels of their temples were wrought of silver and gold. He equipped them with priests and with ritual-priests, and with the choicest of the army. He transferred to them lands and cattle, supplied with all equipment." By these gifts to the neglected gods, Horemheb was striving to bring Egypt back to its normal condition, and in no way was he prejudiced by any particular devotion to Amon.

A certain Patonemheb, who had been one of Akhnaton's favourites in the days of the revolution, was appointed High Priest of Ra—the older Egyptian form of Aton who was at this time identified with that god—at the temple of Heliopolis; and this can only be regarded as an act of friendship to the Aton-worshippers. The echoing and deserted temples of Aton in Thebes, and El Amârna, however, were now pulled down, and the blocks were used for the enlarging of the temple of Amon,—a fact which indicates that their original dedication to Aton had not caused them to be accursed.

The process of restoration was so gradual that it could not have much disturbed the country. Horemheb's hand was firm but soothing in these matters, and the revolution seems to have been killed as much by kindness as by force. It was probably not till quite the end of his reign that he showed any tendency to revile the memory of Akhnaton; and the high feeling which at length brought the revolutionary king the name of "that criminal of El Amârna" did not rise till half a century later. The difficulties experienced by Horemheb in steering his course between Amon and Aton, in quietly restoring the old equilibrium without in any way persecuting those who by religious convictions were Aton-worshippers, must have been immense; and one cannot but feel that the King must have been a diplomatist of the highest standing. His unaffected simplicity won all hearts to him; his toleration and broadness of mind brought all thoughtful men to his train; and his strong will led them and guided them from chaos to order, from fantastic Utopia to the solid old Egypt of the past. Horemheb was the preacher of Sanity, the apostle of the Normal, and Order was his watchword.

The inscriptions tell us that it was his custom to give public audiences to his subjects, and there was not a man amongst those persons whom he interviewed whose name he did not know, nor one who did not leave his presence rejoicing. Up and down the Nile he sailed a hundred times, until he was able truly to say, "I have improved this entire land; I have learned its whole interior; I have travelled it entirely in its midst." We are told that "his Majesty took counsel with his heart how he might expel evil and suppress lying. The plans of his Majesty were an excellent refuge, repelling violence and delivering the Egyptians from the oppressions which were around them. Behold, his Majesty spent the whole time seeking the welfare of Egypt, and searching out instances of oppression in the land."

It is interesting, by the way, to note that in his eighth year the King restored the tomb of Thutmosis IV., which had been robbed during the revolution; and the inscription which the inspectors left behind them was found on the wall when Mr Theodore Davis discovered the tomb a few years ago. The plundering of the royal tombs is a typical instance of the lawlessness of the times. The corruption, too, which followed on the disorder was appalling; and wherever the King went he was confronted by deceit, embezzlement, bribery, extortion, and official tyranny. Every Government officer was attempting to obtain money from his subordinates by illegal means; and *bakshish*—that bogie of the Nile Valley—cast its shadow upon all men.

Horemheb stood this as long as he could; but at last, regarding justice as more necessary than tact, we are told that "his Majesty seized a writing-palette and scroll, and put into writing all that his Majesty the King had said to himself." It is not possible to record here more than a few of the good laws which he then made, but the following examples will serve to show how near to his heart were the interests of his people.

It was the custom for the tax-collectors to place that portion of a farmer's harvest, which they had taken, upon the farmer's own boat, in order to convey it to the public granary. These boats often failed to be returned to their owners when finished with, and were ultimately sold by the officials for their own profit. Horemheb, therefore, made the following law:—

> "If the poor man has made for himself a boat with its sail, and, in order to serve the State, has loaded it with the Government dues, and has been robbed of the boat, the poor man stands bereft of his property and stripped of his many labours. This is wrong, and the Pharaoh will suppress it by his excellent measures. If there be a poor man who pays the taxes to the two deputies, and he be robbed of his property and his boat, my majesty commands: that every officer who collects the taxes and takes the boat of any citizen, this law shall be executed against him, and his nose shall be cut off, and he shall be sent in exile to Tharu. Furthermore, concerning the tax of timber, my majesty commands that if any officer find a poor man without a boat, then he shall bring him a craft belonging to another man in which to carry the timber; and in return for this let the former man do the loading of the timber for the latter."

The tax-collectors were wont to commandeer the services of all the slaves in the town, and to detain them for six or seven days, "so that it was an excessive detention indeed." Often, too, they used to appropriate a portion of the tax for themselves. The new law, therefore, was as follows:—

> "If there be any place where the officials are tax-collecting, and any one shall hear the report saying that they are tax-collecting to take the produce for themselves, and another shall come to report saying, 'My man slave or my female slave has been taken away and detained many days at work by the officials,' the offender's nose shall be cut off, and he shall be sent to Tharu."

One more law may here be quoted. The police used often to steal the hides which the peasants had collected to hand over to the Government as their tax. Horemheb, having satisfied himself that a tale of this kind was not merely an excuse for not paying the tax, made this law:—

> "As for any policeman concerning whom one shall hear it said that he goes about stealing hides, beginning with this day the law shall be executed against him, by beating him a hundred blows, opening five wounds, and taking from him by force the hides which he took."

To carry out these laws he appointed two chief judges of very high standing, who are said to have been "perfect in speech, excellent in good qualities, knowing how to judge the heart." Of these men the King writes: "I have directed them to the way of life, I have led them to the truth, I have taught them, saying, 'Do not receive the reward of another. How, then, shall those like you judge others, while there is one among you committing a crime against justice?'" Under these two officials Horemheb appointed many judges, who went on circuit around the country; and the King took the wise step of arranging, on the one hand, that their pay should be so good that they would not be tempted to take bribes, and, on the other hand, that the penalty for this crime should be most severe.

So many were the King's reforms that one is inclined to forget that he was primarily a soldier. He appears to have made some successful expeditions against the Syrians, but the fighting was probably near his own frontiers, for the empire lost by Akhnaton was not recovered for many years, and Horemheb seems to have felt that Egypt needed to learn to rule herself before she attempted to rule other nations. An expedition against some tribes in the Sudan was successfully carried through, and it is said that "his name was mighty in the land of Kush, his battle-cry was in their dwelling-places." Except for a semi-military expedition which was dispatched to the land of Punt, these are the only recorded foreign activities of the King; but that he had spent much time in the organisation and improvement of the army is shown by the fact that three years after his death the Egyptian soldiers were swarming over the Lebanon and hammering at the doors of the cities of Jezreel.

Had he lived for another few years he might have been famous as a conqueror as well as an administrator, though old age might retard and tired bones refuse their office. As it is, however, his name is written sufficiently large in the book of the world's great men; and when he died, about B.C. 1315, after a reign of some thirty-five years, he had done more for Egypt than had almost any other Pharaoh. He found the country in the wildest disorder, and he left it the master of itself, and ready to become once more the master of the empire which Akhnaton's doctrine of Peace and Goodwill had lost. Under his direction the purged worship of the old gods, which for him meant but the maintenance of some time-proved customs, had gained the mastery over the chimerical worship of Aton; without force or violence he had substituted the practical for the visionary; and to Amon and Order his grateful subjects were able to cry, "The sun of him who knew thee not has set, but he who knows thee shines; the sanctuary of him who assailed thee is overwhelmed in darkness, but the whole earth is now in light."

The tomb of this great Pharaoh was cut in the rocks on the west side of the Valley of the Tombs of the Kings, not far from the resting-place of Amenhotep II. In the days of the later Ramesside kings the tomb-plunderers entered the sepulchre, pulled the embalmed body of the king to pieces in the search for hidden jewels, scattered the bones of the three members of his family who were buried with him, and stole almost everything of value which they found. There must have been other robberies after this, and finally the Government inspectors of about B.C. 1100 entered the tomb, and, seeing its condition, closed its mouth with a compact mass of stones. The torrents of rain which sometimes fall in winter in Egypt percolated through this filling, and left it congealed and difficult to cut through; and on the top of this hard mass tons of rubbish were tossed from other excavations, thus completely hiding the entrance.

In this condition the tomb was found by Mr Davis in February 1908. Mr Davis had been working on the side of the valley opposite to the tomb of Rameses III., where the accumulations of *débris* had entirely hidden the face of the rocks, and, as this was a central and likely spot for a "find," it was hoped that when the skin of rubbish had been cleared away the entrance of at least one royal tomb would be exposed. Of all the XVIIIth-Dynasty kings, the burial-places of only Thutmosis II., Tutankhamon, and Horemheb remained undiscovered, and the hopes of the excavators concentrated on these three Pharaohs.

After a few weeks of digging, the mouth of a large shaft cut into the limestone was cleared. This proved to lead into a small chamber half-filled with rubbish, amongst which some fine jewellery, evidently hidden here, was found. This is now well published by Mr Davis in facsimile, and further mention of it here is unnecessary. Continuing the work, it was not long before traces of another tomb became apparent, and in a few days' time we were able to look down from the surrounding mounds of rubbish upon the commencement of a rectangular cutting in the rock. The size and style of the entrance left no doubt that the work was to be dated to the end of the XVIIIth Dynasty, and the excavators were confident that the tomb of either Tutankhamon or Horemheb lay before them. Steps leading down to the entrance were presently uncovered, and finally the doorway itself was freed from *débris*.

On one of the door-posts an inscription was now seen, written in black ink by one of the Government inspectors of B.C. 1100. This stated, that in the fourth year of an unknown king the tomb had been inspected, and had been found to be that of Horemheb.

PL. XXII. The mouth of the tomb of Horemheb at the time of its discovery. The author is seen emerging from the tomb after the first entrance had been effected. On the hillside the workmen are grouped.
*[Photo by Lady Glyn.]*

We had hoped now to pass into the tomb without further difficulty, but in this we were disappointed, for the first corridor was quite choked with the rubbish placed there by the inspectors. This corridor led down at a steep angle through the limestone hillside, and, like all other parts of the tomb, it was carefully worked. It was not until two days later that enough clearing had been done to allow us to crawl in over the rubbish, which was still piled up so nearly to the roof that there was only just room to wriggle downwards over it with our backs pressing against the stone above. At the lower end of the corridor there was a flight of steps towards which the rubbish shelved, and, sliding down the slope, we were here able to stand once more. It was obvious that the tomb did not stop here, and work, therefore, had to be begun on the rubbish which choked the stairway in order to expose the entrance to further passages. A doorway soon became visible, and at last this was sufficiently cleared to permit of our crawling into the next corridor, though now we were even more closely squeezed between the roof and the *débris* than before.

The party which made the entrance consisted of Mr Davis; his assistant, Mr Ayrton; Mr Harold Jones; Mr Max Dalison, formerly of the Egypt Exploration Fund; and myself. Wriggling and crawling, we pushed and pulled ourselves down the sloping rubbish, until, with a rattling avalanche of small stones, we arrived at the bottom of the passage, where we scrambled to our feet at the brink of a large rectangular well, or shaft. Holding the lamps aloft, the surrounding walls were seen to be covered with wonderfully preserved paintings executed on slightly raised plaster. Here Horemheb was seen standing before Isis, Osiris, Horus, and other gods; and his cartouches stood out boldly from amidst the elaborate inscriptions. The colours were extremely rich, and, though there was so much to be seen ahead, we stood there for some minutes, looking at them with a feeling much akin to awe.

The shaft was partly filled with rubbish, and not being very deep, we were able to climb down it by means of a ladder, and up the other side to an entrance which formed a kind of window in the sheer wall. In entering a large tomb for the first time, there are one or two scenes which fix themselves upon the memory more forcefully than others, and one feels as though one might carry these impressions intact to the grave. In this tomb there was nothing so impressive as this view across the well and through the entrance in the opposite wall. At one's feet lay the dark pit; around one the gaudy paintings gleamed; and through the window-like aperture before one, a dim suggestion could be obtained of a white-pillared hall. The intense eagerness to know what was beyond, and, at the same time, the feeling that it was almost desecration to climb into those halls which had stood silent for thousands of years, cast a spell over the scene and made it unforgetable.

This aperture had once been blocked up with stones, and the paintings had passed across it, thus hiding it from view, so that a robber entering the tomb might think that it ended here. But the trick was an old one, and the plunderers had easily detected the entrance, had pulled away the blocks, and had climbed through. Following in their footsteps, we went up the ladder and passed through the entrance into the pillared hall. Parts of the roof had fallen in, and other parts appeared to be likely to do so at any moment. Clambering over the *débris* we descended another sloping corridor, which was entered through a cutting in the floor of the hall, originally blocked up and hidden. This brought us into a chamber covered with paintings, like those around the well; and again we were brought to a standstill by the amazingly fresh colours which arrested and held the attention.

We then passed on into the large burial-hall, the roof of which was supported by crumbling pillars. Slabs of limestone had broken off here and there and had crashed down on to the floor, bringing with them portions of the ceiling painted with a design of yellow stars on a black ground. On the walls were unfinished paintings, and it was interesting to notice that the north, south, east, and west were clearly marked upon the four walls for ceremonial purposes.

The main feature towards which our eyes were turned was the great pink-granite sarcophagus which stood in the middle of the hall. Its sides were covered with well-cut inscriptions of a religious nature; and at the four corners there were figures of Isis and Nephthys, in relief, with their wings spread out as though in protection around the body. Looking into the sarcophagus, the lid having been thrown off by the plunderers, we found it empty except for a skull and a few bones of more than one person. The sarcophagus stood upon the limestone floor, and under it small holes had been cut, in each of which a little wooden statue of a god had been placed. Thus the king's body was, so to speak, carried on the heads of the gods, and held aloft by their arms. This is a unique arrangement, and has never before been found in any burial.

In all directions broken figures of the gods were lying, and two defaced wooden statues of the king were overthrown beside the sarcophagus. Beautiful pieces of furniture, such as were found by Mr Davis in the tomb of Yuaa and Thuau, were not to be expected in the sepulchre of a Pharaoh; for whereas those two persons were only mortals and required mortal comforts in the Underworld, the king was a god and needed only the comfort of the presence of other gods. Dead flowers were found here and there amidst the *débris*, these being the remnant of the masses of garlands which were always heaped around and over the coffin.

Peering into a little chamber on the right, we saw two skulls and some broken bones lying in the corner. These appeared to be female, and one of the skulls may have been that of Mutnezem, the queen. In another small chamber on the left there was a fine painting of Osiris on the back wall; and, crouching at the foot of this, a statuette of a god with upraised hands had been placed. As we turned the corner and came upon it in the full glare of the lamps, one felt that the arms were raised in horror at sight of us, and that the god was gasping with surprise and indignation at our arrival. In the floor of another ante-chamber a square hole was cut, leading down to a small room. A block of stone had neatly fitted over the opening, thus hiding it from view; but the robbers had detected the crack, and had found the hiding-place. Here there were a skull and a few bones, again of more than one person. Altogether there must have been four bodies buried in the tomb; and it seems that the inspectors, finding them strewn in all directions, had replaced one skull in the sarcophagus, two in the side room, and one in this hiding-place, dividing up the bones between these three places as they thought fit. It may be that the king himself was buried in the underground chamber, and that the sarcophagus was a sort of blind; for he had seen the destruction caused by robbers in the tomb of Thutmosis IV., which he had restored, and he may have made this attempt to secure the safety of his own body. Whether this be so or not, however, Fate has not permitted the body of the great king to escape the hands of the destroyer, and it will now never be known with certainty whether one of these four heads wore the crown of the Pharaohs.

The temperature was very great in the tomb, and the perspiration streamed down our faces as we stood contemplating the devastation. Now the electric lamps would flash upon the gods supporting the ransacked sarcophagus, lighting for a moment their grotesque forms; now the attention would concentrate upon some wooden figure of a hippopotamus-god or cow-headed deity; and now the light would bring into prominence the great overthrown statue of the king. There is something peculiarly sensational in the examining of a tomb which has not been entered for such thousands of years, but it must be left to the imaginative reader to infuse a touch of that feeling of the dramatic into these words. It would be hopeless to attempt to put into writing those impressions which go to make the entering of a great Egyptian sepulchre so thrilling an experience: one cannot describe the silence, the echoing steps, the dark shadows, the hot, breathless air; nor tell of the sense of vast Time the penetrating of it which stirs one so deeply.

The air was too bad to permit of our remaining long so deep in the bowels of the earth; and we presently made our way through halls and corridors back to the upper world, scrambling and crashing over the *débris*, and squeezing ourselves through the rabbit-hole by which we had entered. As we passed out of this hot, dark tomb into the brilliant sunlight and the bracing north wind, the gloomy wreck of the place was brought before the imagination with renewed force. The scattered bones, the broken statues, the dead flowers, grouped themselves in the mind into a picture of utter decay. In some of the tombs which have been opened the freshness of the objects has caused one to exclaim at the inaction of the years; but here, where vivid and well-preserved wall-paintings looked down on a jumbled collection of smashed fragments of wood and bones, one felt how hardly the Powers deal with the dead. How far away seemed the great fight between Amon and Aton; how futile the task which Horemheb accomplished so gloriously! It was all over and forgotten, and one asked oneself what it mattered whether the way was difficult or the battle slow to win. In the fourth year of the reign of Horemheb a certain harper named Neferhotep partly composed a song which was peculiarly appropriate to the tune which ran in one's head at the opening of the tomb of this Pharaoh whom the harper served—

> "(1.) Behold the dwellings of the dead. Their walls fall down; their place is no more: they are as though they had never existed. (2.) That which hath come into being must pass away again. The young men and maidens go to their places; the sun riseth at dawn, and setteth again in the hills of the west. Men beget and women conceive. The children, too, go to the places which are appointed for them. O, then, be happy! Come, scents and perfumes are set before thee: *mahu*-flowers and lilies for the arms and neck of thy beloved. Come, songs and music are before thee. Set behind thee all cares; think only upon gladness, until that day cometh whereon thou shalt go down to the land which loveth silence."

Horemheb must often have heard this song sung in his palace at Thebes by its composer; but did he think, one wonders, that it would be the walls of his own tomb which would fall down, and his own bones which would be almost as though they had never existed?

# PART IV.

# THE PRESERVATION OF THE TREASURY.

"Laugh and mock if you will at the worship of stone idols, but mark ye this, ye breakers of images, that in one regard the stone idol bears awful semblance of Deity—the unchangefulness in the midst of change—the same seeming will, and intent for ever and ever inexorable! . . . And we, we shall die, and Islam will wither away, and the Englishman straining far over to hold his loved India, will plant a firm foot on the banks of the Nile and sit in the seats of the Faithful, and still that sleepless rock will lie watching and watching the works of the new busy race, with those same sad earnest eyes, and the same tranquil mien everlastingly."

—KINGLAKE: *Eothen* (1844).

# CHAPTER X.

## THEBAN THIEVES.

Thebes was the ancient capital of Egypt, and its ruins are the most extensive in the Nile Valley. On the east bank of the river, at the modern towns of Luxor and Karnak, there are the remains of mighty temples; and on the west bank, in the neighbourhood of the village of Gurneh, tombs, mortuary chapels, and temples, literally cover the ground. The inhabitants of these three places have for generations augmented their incomes by a traffic in antiquities, and the peasants of Gurneh have, more especially, become famous as the most hardy pilferers of the tombs of their ancestors in all Egypt. In conducting this lucrative business they have lately had the misfortune to be recognised as thieves and robbers by the Government, and it is one of my duties to point this out to them. As a matter of fact they are no more thieves than you or I. It is as natural for them to scratch in the sand for antiquities as it is for us to pick flowers by the roadside: antiquities, like flowers, are the product of the soil, and it is largely because the one is more rare than the other that its promiscuous appropriation has been constituted an offence. The native who is sometimes child enough to put his eyes out rather than serve in the army, who will often suffer all manner of wrongs rather than carry his case to the local courts, and who will hide his money under his bed rather than trust it to the safest bank, is not likely to be intelligent enough to realise that, on scientific grounds, he is committing a crime in digging for scarabs. He is beginning to understand that in the eyes of the law he is a criminal, but he has not yet learnt so to regard himself. I here name him thief, for officially that is his designation; but there is no sting in the word, nor is any insult intended. By all cultured persons the robbery of antiquities must be regarded as a grave offence, and one which has to be checked. But the point is ethical; and what has the Theban to do with ethics? The robbery of antiquities is carried out in many different ways and from many different motives. Sometimes it is romantic treasure hunting that the official has to deal with; sometimes it is adventurous robbery with violence; sometimes it is the taking advantage of chance discoveries; sometimes it is the pilfering of objects found in authorised excavations; and sometimes it is the stealing of fragments smashed from the walls of the ancient monuments. All these forms of robbery, except the last, may call for the sympathy of every reader of these lines who happens not to have cultivated that vaguely defined "archæological sense" which is, practically, the product of this present generation alone; and in the instances which are here to be given the point of view of the "Theban thief" will be readily appreciated.

PL. XXIII. A modern Theban Fellah-woman and her child.
*[Photo by E. Bird.]*

Treasure hunting is a relic of childhood that remains, like all other forms of romance and adventure, a permanently youthful feature in our worn old hearts. It has been drilled into us by the tales of our boyhood, and, in later life, it has become part of that universal desire to get something for nothing which lies behind our most honest efforts to obtain the goods of this world. Who has not desired the hidden wealth of the late Captain Kidd, or coveted the lost treasure of the Incas? I recently wrote an article which was entitled "Excavations in Egypt," but the editor of the magazine in which it appeared hastily altered these words to "Treasure Hunting in Egypt," and thereby commanded the attention of twice the number of readers. Can we wonder, then, that this form of adventure is so often met with in Egypt, the land of hidden treasure? The Department of Antiquities has lately published a collection of mediæval traditions with regard to this subject, which is known as the Book of the Pearl. In it one is told the exact places where excavations should be made to lay bare the wealth of the ancients. "Go to such and such a spot," says this curious book, "and dig to the depth of so many cubits, and you will find a trap-door; descend through this and you will find a chamber wherein are forty jars filled with gold. Take what you want, and give thanks to God." Many of the sites referred to have been literally hacked out of all recognition by the picks and spades of thousands of gold-seekers; and it may be that sometimes their efforts have been rewarded, since a certain amount of genuine information is embodied in the traditions. Sir Gaston Maspero, the Director-General of the Department of Antiquities, tells a story of how a native came to him asking permission to excavate at a certain spot where he believed treasure to be hidden. Sir Gaston accompanied him to the place, and a tunnel was bored into what appeared to be virgin sand and rock. At the end of the first day's work the futility of his labours was pointed out to the man, but he was not to be daunted. For two more days he stood watching the work from morn to nightfall with hope burning in his eyes, and on the following morning his reward came. Suddenly the ground gave way before the picks of the workmen, and a hole was seen leading into a forgotten cave. In this cave the implements of mediæval coiners were discovered, and an amount of metal, false and true, was found which had been used by them in the process of their business.

A short time ago a man applied for permission to perform a similar kind of excavation at a place called Nag Hamadi, and in my absence permission was given him. On my return the following report was submitted: ". . . Having reached the spot indicated the man started to blow the stones by means of the Denamits. Also he slaught a lamb, thinking that there is a treasure, and that when the lamb being slaught he will discover it at once." In plainer English, the man had blown up the rocks with dynamite, and had attempted to further his efforts by sacrificing a lamb to the *djin* who guarded the treasure. The *djin*, however, was not thus to be propitiated, and the gold of the Pharaohs was never found. More recently the watchmen of the famous temple of Dêr el Bahri found themselves in trouble owing to the discovery that part of the ancient pavement showed signs of having been raised, stone by stone, in order that the ground below might be searched for the treasure which a tradition, such as those in the Book of the Pearl, had reported as lying hid there.

Almost as romantic as treasure hunting is robbery with violence. We all remember our boyhood's fascination for piracy, smuggling, and the profession of Dick Turpin; and to the Theban peasant, who is essentially youthful in his ideas, this form of fortune hunting has irresistible attractions. When a new tomb is discovered by authorised archæologists, especially when it is situated in some remote spot such as the Valley of the Kings, there is always some fear of an armed raid; and police guard the spot night and day until the antiquities have been removed to Cairo. The workmen who have been employed in the excavation return to their homes with wonderful tales of the wealth which the tomb contains, and in the evening the discovery is discussed by the women at the well where the water is drawn for the village, with the result that it very soon assumes prodigious proportions, inflaming the minds of all men with the greed of gold. Visitors often ask why it is that the mummies of the Pharaohs are not left to lie each in its own tomb; and it is argued that they look neither congruous nor dignified in the glass cases of the museum. The answer is obvious to all who know the country: put them back in their tombs, and, without continuous police protection, they will be broken into fragments by robbers, bolts and bars notwithstanding. The experiment of leaving the mummy and some of the antiquities *in situ* has only once been tried, and it has not been a complete success. It was done in the case of the tomb of Amenhotep II. at Thebes, the mummy being laid in its original sarcophagus; and a model boat, used in one of the funeral ceremonies, was left in the tomb. One night the six watchmen who were in charge of the royal tombs stated that they had been attacked by an armed force; the tomb in question was seen to have been entered, the iron doors having been forced. The mummy of the Pharaoh was found lying upon the floor of the burial-hall, its chest smashed in; and the boat had disappeared, nor has it since been recovered. The watchmen showed signs of having put up something of a fight, their clothes being riddled with bullet-holes; but here and there the cloth looked much as though it had been singed, which suggested, as did other evidence, that they themselves had fired the guns and had acted the struggle. The truth of the matter will never be known, but its lesson is obvious. The mummy was put back into its sarcophagus, and there it has remained secure ever since; but one never knows how soon it will be dragged forth once more to be searched for the gold with which every native thinks it is stuffed.

Some years ago an armed gang walked off with a complete series of mortuary reliefs belonging to a tomb at Sakkârah. They came by night, overpowered the watchmen, loaded the blocks of stone on to camels, and disappeared into the darkness. Sometimes it is an entire cemetery that is attacked; and, if it happens to be situated some miles from the nearest police-station, a good deal of work can be done before the authorities get wind of the affair. Last winter six hundred men set to work upon a patch of desert ground where a tomb had been accidently found, and, ere I received the news, they had robbed a score of little graves, many of which must have contained objects purchasable by the dealers in antiquities for quite large sums of money. At Abydos a tomb which we had just discovered was raided by the villagers, and we only regained possession of it after a rapid exchange of shots, one of which came near ending a career whose continuance had been, since birth, a matter of great importance to myself. But how amusing the adventure must have been for the raiders!

The appropriation of treasure-trove come upon by chance, or the digging out of graves accidentally discovered, is a very natural form of robbery for the natives to indulge in, and one which commends itself to the sympathies of all those not actively concerned in its suppression. There are very few persons even in western countries who would be willing to hand over to the Government a hoard of gold discovered in their own back garden. In Egypt the law is that the treasure-trove thus discovered belongs to the owner of the property; and thus there is always a certain amount of excavation going on behind the walls of the houses. It is also the law that the peasants may carry away the accumulated rubbish on the upper layers of ancient town sites, in order to use it as a fertiliser for their crops, since it contains valuable phosphates. This work is supervised by watchmen, but this does not prevent the stealing of almost all the antiquities which are found. As illegal excavators these *sebakhîn*, or manure-diggers, are the worst offenders, for they search for the phosphates in all manner of places, and are constantly coming upon tombs or ruins which they promptly clear of their contents. One sees them driving their donkeys along the roads, each laden with a sack of manure, and it is certain that some of these sacks contain antiquities. In Thebes many of the natives live inside the tombs of the ancient nobles, these generally consisting of two or three rock-hewn halls from which a tunnel leads down to the burial-chamber. Generally this tunnel is choked with *débris*, and the owner of the house will perhaps come upon it by chance, and will dig it out, in the vain hope that earlier plunderers have left some of the antiquities undisturbed. It recently happened that an entire family was asphyxiated while attempting to penetrate into a newly discovered tunnel, each member entering to ascertain the fate of the previous explorer, and each being overcome by the gases. On one occasion I was asked by a native to accompany him down a tunnel, the entrance of which was in his stable, in order to view a sarcophagus which lay at the bottom. We each took a candle, and, crouching down to avoid the low roof, we descended the narrow, winding passage, the loose stones sliding beneath our feet. The air was very foul; and below us there was the thunderous roar of thousands of wings beating through the echoing passage—the wings of evil-smelling bats. Presently we reached this uncomfortable zone. So thickly did the bats hang from the ceiling that the rock itself seemed to be black; but as we advanced, and the creatures took to their wings, this black covering appeared to peel off the rock. During the entire descent this curious spectacle of regularly receding blackness and advancing grey was to be seen a yard or so in front of us. The roar of wings was now deafening, for the space into which we were driving the bats was very confined. My guide shouted to me that we must let them pass out of the tomb over our heads. We therefore crouched down, and a few stones were flung into the darkness ahead. Then, with a roar and a rush of air, they came, bumping into us, entangling themselves in our clothes, slapping our faces and hands with their unwholesome wings, and clinging to our fingers. At last the thunder died away in the passage behind us, and we were able to advance more easily, though the ground was alive with the bats maimed in the frantic flight which had taken place, floundering out of our way and squeaking shrilly. The sarcophagus proved to be of no interest, so the encounter with the bats was to no purpose.

The pilfering of antiquities found during the course of authorised excavations is one of the most common forms of robbery. The overseer cannot always watch the workmen sufficiently closely to prevent them pocketing the small objects which they find, and it is an easy matter to carry off the stolen goods, even though the men are searched at the end of the day. A little girl minding her father's sheep and goats in the neighbourhood of the excavations, and apparently occupying her hands with the spinning of flax, is perhaps the receiver of the objects. Thus it is more profitable to dig for antiquities even in authorised excavations than to work the water-hoist, which is one of the usual occupations of the peasant. Pulling the hoisting-pole down, and swinging it up again with its load of water many thousands of times in the day, is monotonous work; whereas digging in the ground, with the eyes keenly watching for the appearance of antiquities, is always interesting and exciting. And why should the digger refrain from appropriating the objects which his pick reveals? If he does not make use of his opportunities and carry off the antiquities, the western director of the works will take them to his own country and sell them for his own profit. All natives believe that the archæologists work for the purpose of making money. Speaking of Professor Flinders Petrie, a peasant said to me the other day: "He has worked five-and-twenty years now; he must be *very* rich." He would never believe that the antiquities were given to museums without any payment being made to the finder.

The stealing of fragments broken out of the walls of "show" monuments is almost the only form of robbery which will receive general condemnation. That this vandalism is also distasteful to the natives themselves is shown by the fact that several better-class Egyptians living in the neighbourhood of Thebes subscribed, at my invitation, the sum of £50 for the protection of certain beautiful tombs. When they were shown the works undertaken with their money, they expressed themselves as being "pleased with the delicate inscriptions in the tombs, but very awfully angry at the damage which the devils of ignorant people had made." A native of moderate intelligence can quite appreciate the argument that whereas the continuous warfare between the agents of the Department of Antiquities and the illegal excavators of small graves is what might be called an honourable game, the smashing of public monuments cannot be called fair-play from whatever point of view the matter is approached. Often revenge or spite is the cause of this damage. It is sometimes necessary to act with severity to the peasants who infringe the rules of the Department, but a serious danger lies in such action, for it is the nature of the Thebans to revenge themselves not on the official directly but on the monuments which he is known to love. Two years ago a native illegally built himself a house on Government ground, and I was obliged to go through the formality of pulling it down, which I did by obliging him to remove a few layers of brickwork around the walls. A short time afterwards a famous tomb was broken into and a part of the paintings destroyed; and there was enough evidence to show that the owner of this house was the culprit, though unfortunately he could not be convicted. One man actually had the audacity to warn me that any severity on my part would be met by destruction of monuments. Under these circumstances an official finds himself in a dilemma. If he maintains the dignity and prestige of his Department by punishing any offences against it, he endangers the very objects for the care of which he is responsible; and it is hard to say whether under a lax or a severe administration the more damage would be done.

PL. XXIV. A modern Gournawi beggar.
*[Photo by E. Bird.]*

The produce of these various forms of robbery is easily disposed of. When once the antiquities have passed into the hands of the dealers there is little chance of further trouble. The dealer can always say that he came into possession of an object years ago, before the antiquity laws were made, and it is almost impossible to prove that he did not. You may have the body of a statue and he the head: he can always damage the line of the breakage, and say that the head does not belong to that statue, or, if the connection is too obvious, he can say that he found the head while excavating twenty years ago on the site where now you have found the body. Nor is it desirable to bring an action against the man in a case of this kind, for it might go against the official. Dealing in antiquities is regarded as a perfectly honourable business. The official, crawling about the desert on his stomach in the bitter cold of a winter's night in order to hold up a convoy of stolen antiquities, may use hard language in regard to the trade, but he cannot say that it is pernicious as long as it is confined to minor objects. How many objects of value to science would be destroyed by their finders if there was no market to take them to! One of the Theban dealers leads so holy a life that he will assuredly be regarded as a saint by future generations.

The sale of small antiquities to tourists on the public roads is prohibited, except at certain places, but of course it can be done with impunity by the exercise of a little care. Men and boys and even little girls as they pass will stare at you with studying eyes, and if you seem to be a likely purchaser, they will draw from the folds of their garments some little object which they will offer for sale. Along the road in the glory of the setting sun there will come as fine a young man as you will see on a day's march. Surely he is bent on some noble mission: what lofty thoughts are occupying his mind, you wonder. But as you pass, out comes the scarab from his pocket, and he shouts, "Wanty scarab, mister?—two shillin'," while you ride on your way a greater cynic than before.

Some years ago a large inscribed stone was stolen from a certain temple, and was promptly sold to a man who sometimes traded in such objects. This man carried the stone, hidden in a sack of grain, to the house of a friend, and having deposited it in a place of hiding, he tramped home, with his stick across his shoulders, in an attitude of deep unconcern. An enemy of his, however, had watched him, and promptly gave information. Acting on this the police set out to search the house. When we reached the entrance we were met by the owner, and a warrant was shown to him. A heated argument followed, at the end of which the infuriated man waved us in with a magnificent and most dramatic gesture. There were some twenty rooms in the house, and the stifling heat of a July noon made the task none too enjoyable. The police inspector was extremely thorough in his work, and an hour had passed before three rooms had been searched. He looked into the cupboards, went down on his knees to peer into the ovens, stood on tiptoe to search the fragile wooden shelves (it was a heavy stone which we were looking for), hunted under the mats, and even peeped into a little tobacco-tin. In one of the rooms there were three or four beds arranged along the middle of the floor. The inspector pulled off the mattresses, and out from under each there leapt a dozen rats, which, if I may be believed, made for the walls and ran straight up them, disappearing in the rafter-holes at the top. The sight of countless rats hurrying up perpendicular walls may be familiar to some people, but I venture to call it an amazing spectacle, worthy of record. Then came the opening of one or two travelling-trunks. The inspector ran his hand through the clothes which lay therein, and out jumped a few more rats, which likewise went up the walls. The searching of the remaining rooms carried us well through the afternoon; and at last, hot and weary, we decided to abandon the hunt. Two nights later a man was seen walking away from the house with a heavy sack on his back; and the stone is now, no doubt, in the Western hemisphere.

The attempt to regain a lost antiquity is seldom crowned with success. It is so extremely difficult to obtain reliable information; and as soon as a man is suspected his enemies will rush in with accusations. Thirty-eight separate accusations were sent in against a certain head-watchman during the first days after the fact had leaked out that he was under suspicion. Not one of them could be shown to be true. Sometimes one man will bring a charge against another for the betterment of his own interests.

Here is a letter from a watchman who had resigned, but wished to rejoin, "To his Exec. Chief Dircoter of the tembels. I have honner to inform that I am your servant X, watchman on the tembels before this time. Sir from one year ago I work in the Santruple (?) as a watchman about four years ago. And I not make anything wrong and your Exec. know me. Now I want to work in my place in the tembel, because the man which in it he not attintive to His, but alway he in the coffee . . . He also steal the scribed stones. Please give your order to point me again. Your servant, X." "The coffee" is, of course, the *café* which adjoins the temple.

A short time ago a young man came to me with an accusation against his own father, who, he said, had stolen a statuette. The tale which he told was circumstantial, but it was hotly denied by his infuriated parent. He looked, however, a trifle more honest than his father, and when a younger brother was brought in as witness, one felt that the guilt of the old man would be the probable finding. The boy stared steadfastly at the ground for some moments, however, and then launched out into an elaborate explanation of the whole affair. He said that he asked his father to lend him four pounds, but the father had refused. The son insisted that that sum was due to him as his share in some transaction, and pointed out that though he only asked for it as a loan, he had in reality a claim to it. The old man refused to hand it over, and the son, therefore, waited his opportunity and stole it from his house, carrying it off triumphantly to his own establishment. Here he gave it into the charge of his young wife, and went about his business. The father, however, guessed where the money had gone; and while his son was out, invaded his house, beat his daughter-in-law on the soles of her feet until she confessed where the money was hidden, and then, having obtained it, returned to his home. When the son came back to his house he learnt what had happened, and, out of spite, at once invented the accusation which he had brought to me. This story appeared to be true in so far as the quarrel over the money was concerned, but that the accusation was invented proved to be untrue.

Sometimes the peasants have such honest faces that it is difficult to believe that they are guilty of deceit. A lady came to the camp of a certain party of excavators at Thebes, holding in her hand a scarab. "Do tell me," she said to one of the archæologists, "whether this scarab is genuine. I am sure it must be, for I bought it from a boy who assured me that he had stolen it from your excavations, and he looked such an honest and truthful little fellow."

In order to check pilfering in a certain excavation in which I was assisting we made a rule that the selected workmen should not be allowed to put unselected substitutes in their place. One day I came upon a man whose appearance did not seem familiar, although his back was turned to me. I asked him who he was, whereupon he turned upon me a countenance which might have served for the model of a painting of St John, and in a low, sweet-voice he told me of the illness of the real workman, and of how he had taken over the work in order to obtain money for the purchase of medicine for him, they being friends from their youth up. I sent him away and told him to call for any medicine he might want that evening. I did not see him again until about a week later, when I happened to meet him in the village with a policeman on either side of him, from one of whom I learned that he was a well-known thief. Thus is one deceived even in the case of real criminals: how then can one expect to get at the truth when the crime committed is so light an affair as the stealing of an antiquity?

The following is a letter received from one of the greatest thieves in Thebes, who is now serving a term of imprisonment in the provincial gaol:—

> "SIR GENERAL INSPECTOR,—I offer this application stating that I am from the natives of Gurneh, saying the following:—
>
> 'On Saturday last I came to your office and have been told that my family using the sate to strengthen against the Department.

The result of this talking that all these things which somebody pretends are not the fact. In fact I am taking great care of the antiquities for the purpose of my living matter. Accordingly, I wish to be appointed in the vacant of watching to the antiquities in my village and promise myself that if anything happens I do hold myself resposible.'"

I have no idea what "using the sate to strengthen" means.

It is sometimes said that European excavators are committing an offence against the sensibilities of the peasants by digging up the bodies of their ancestors. Nobody will repeat this remark who has walked over a cemetery plundered by the natives themselves. Here bodies may be seen lying in all directions, torn limb from limb by the gold-seekers; here beautiful vases may be seen smashed to atoms in order to make more rare the specimens preserved. The peasant has no regard whatsoever for the sanctity of the ancient dead, nor does any superstition in this regard deter him in his work of destruction. Fortunately superstition sometimes checks other forms of robbery. *Djins* are believed to guard the hoards of ancient wealth which some of the tombs are thought to contain, as, for example, in the case of the tomb in which the family was asphyxiated, where a fiend of this kind was thought to have throttled the unfortunate explorers. Twin brothers are thought to have the power of changing themselves into cats at will; and a certain Huseyn Osman, a harmless individual enough, and a most expert digger, would turn himself into a cat at night-time, not only for the purpose of stealing his brother Muhammed Osman's dinner, but also in order to protect the tombs which his patron was occupied in excavating. One of the overseers in some recent excavations was said to have power of detecting all robberies on his works. The archæologist, however, is unfortunately unable to rely upon this form of protection, and many are the schemes for the prevention of pilfering which are tried.

In some excavations a sum of money is given to the workman for every antiquity found by him, and these sums are sufficiently high to prevent any outbidding by the dealers. Work thus becomes very expensive for the archæologist, who is sometimes called upon to pay £10 or £20 in a day. The system has also another disadvantage, namely, that the workmen are apt to bring antiquities from far and near to "discover" in their diggings in order to obtain a good price for them. Nevertheless, it would seem to be the most successful of the systems. In the Government excavations it is usual to employ a number of overseers to watch for the small finds, while for only the really valuable discoveries is a reward given.

For finding the famous gold hawk's head at Hieraconpolis a workman received £14, and with this princely sum in his pocket he went to a certain Englishman to ask advice as to the spending of it. He was troubled, he said, to decide whether to buy a wife or a cow. He admitted that he had already one wife, and that two of them would be sure to introduce some friction into what was now a peaceful household; and he quite realised that a cow would be less apt to quarrel with his first wife. The Englishman, very properly, voted for the cow, and the peasant returned home deep in thought. While pondering over the matter during the next few weeks, he entertained his friends with some freedom, and soon he found to his dismay that he had not enough money left to buy either a wife or a cow. Thereupon he set to with a will, and soon spent the remaining guineas in riotous living. When he was next seen by the Englishman he was a beggar, and, what was worse, his taste for evil living had had several weeks of cultivation.

The case of the fortunate finder of a certain great *cache* of mummies was different. He received a reward of £400, and this he buried in a very secret place. When he died his possessions descended to his sons. After the funeral they sat round the grave of the old man, and very rightly discussed his virtues until the sun set. Then they returned to the house and began to dig for the hidden money. For some days they turned the sand of the floor over; but failing to find what they sought, they commenced operations on a patch of desert under the shade of some tamarisks where their father was wont to sit of an afternoon. It is said that for twelve hours they worked like persons possessed, the men hacking at the ground, and the boys carrying away the sand in baskets to a convenient distance. But the money was never found.

It is not often that the finders of antiquities inform the authorities of their good fortune, but when they do so an attempt is made to give them a good reward. A letter from the finder of an inscribed statue, who wished to claim his reward, read as follows: "With all delight I please inform you that on 8th Jan. was found a headless temple of granite sitting on a chair and printed on it."

I will end this chapter as I began it, in the defence of the Theban thieves. In a place where every yard of ground contains antiquities, and where these antiquities may be so readily converted into golden guineas, can one wonder that every man, woman, and child makes use of his opportunities in this respect to better his fortune? The peasant does not take any interest in the history of mankind, and he cannot be expected to know that in digging out a grave and scattering its contents, through the agency of dealers, over the face of the globe, he loses for ever the facts which the archæologist is striving so hard to obtain. The scientific excavator does not think the antiquities themselves so valuable as the record of the exact arrangement in which they were found. From such data alone can he obtain his knowledge of the manners and customs of this wonderful people. When two objects are found together, the date of one being known and that of the other unknown, the archæological value of the find lies in the fact that the former will place the latter in its correct chronological position. But if these two objects are sold separately, the find may perhaps lose its entire significance. The trained archæologist records every atom of information with which he meets; the native records nothing. And hence, if there is any value at all in the study of the history of mankind, illegal excavation must be stopped.

# CHAPTER XI.

## THE FLOODING OF LOWER NUBIA.

The country of Lower Nubia lies between the First and Second Cataracts of the Nile. The town of Aswan, once famous as the frontier outpost of Egypt and now renowned as a winter resort for Europeans and Americans, stands some two or three miles below the First Cataract; and two hundred miles southwards, at the foot of the Second Cataract, stands Wady Halfa. About half-way between these two points the little town of Derr nestles amidst its palms; and here the single police-station of the province is situated. Agriculturally the land is extremely barren, for the merest strip of cultivation borders the river, and in many reaches the desert comes down to the water's edge. The scenery is rugged and often magnificent. As one sails up the Nile the rocky hills on either side group themselves into bold compositions, rising darkly above the palms and acacias reflected in the water. The villages, clustered on the hillsides as though grown like mushrooms in the night, are not different in colour to the ground upon which they are built; but here and there neatly whitewashed houses of considerable size are to be observed. Now we come upon a tract of desert sand which rolls down to the river in a golden slope; now the hills recede, leaving an open bay wherein there are patches of cultivated ground reclaimed from the wilderness; and now a dense but narrow palm-grove follows the line of the bank for a mile or more, backed by the villages at the foot of the hills.

The inhabitants are few in number. Most of the males have taken service as cooks, butlers, waiters, and bottle-washers in European houses or hotels throughout Egypt; and consequently one sees more women than men pottering about the villages or working in the fields. They are a fine race, clean in their habits and cheery in character. They can be distinguished with ease from the Egyptian *fellahîn*; for their skin has more the appearance of bronze, and their features are often more aquiline. The women do not wear the veil, and their dresses are draped over one shoulder in a manner unknown to Egypt. The method of dressing the hair, moreover, is quite distinctive: the women plait it in innumerable little strands, those along the forehead terminating in bead-like lumps of bee's-wax. The little children go nude for the first six or eight years of their life, though the girls sometimes wear around their waists a fringe made of thin strips of hide. The men still carry spears in some parts of the country, and a light battle-axe is not an uncommon weapon.

There is no railway between Aswan and Halfa, all traffic being conducted on the river. Almost continuously a stream of native troops and English officers passes up and down the Nile bound for Khartoum or Cairo; and in the winter the tourists on steamers and *dahabiyehs* travel through the country in considerable numbers to visit the many temples which were here erected in the days when the land was richer than it is now. The three most famous ruins of Lower Nubia are those of Philae, just above Aswan; Kalabsheh, some forty miles to the south; and Abu Simbel, about thirty miles below Halfa: but besides these there are many buildings of importance and interest. The ancient remains date from all periods of Egyptian history; for Lower Nubia played an important part in Pharaonic affairs, both by reason of its position as the buffer state between Egypt and the Sudan, and also because of its gold-mining industries. In old days it was divided into several tribal states, these being governed by the Egyptian Viceroy of Ethiopia; but the country seldom revolted or gave trouble, and to the present day it retains its reputation for peacefulness and orderly behaviour.

Owing to the building, and now the heightening, of the great Nile dam at Aswan, erected for the purpose of regulating the flow of water by holding back in the plenteous autumn and winter the amount necessary to keep up the level in the dry summer months, the whole of the valley from the First Cataract to the neighbourhood of Derr will be turned into a vast reservoir, and a large number of temples and other ruins will be flooded. Before the dam was finished the temples on the island of Philae were strengthened and repaired so as to be safe from damage by the water; and now every other ruin whose foundations are below the future high-water level has been repaired and safeguarded.

In 1906 and 1907 the present writer was dispatched to the threatened territory to make a full report on the condition of the monuments there;[1] and a very large sum of money was then voted for the work. Sir Gaston Maspero took the matter up in the spirit which is associated with his name; Monsieur Barsanti was sent to repair and underpin the temples; French, German, and English scholars were engaged to make copies of the endangered inscriptions and reliefs; and Dr Reisner, Mr C. Firth, and others, under the direction of Captain Lyons, were entrusted with the complete and exhaustive excavation of all the cemeteries and remains between the dam and the southern extremity of the reservoir. As a result of this work, not one scrap of information of any kind will be lost by the flooding of the country.

As was to be expected, the building and raising of the dam caused consternation amongst the archæologically interested visitors to Egypt, and very considerably troubled the Egyptologists. Philae, one of the most picturesque ruins on the Nile, was to be destroyed, said the more hysterical, and numerous other buildings were to meet with the same fate. A very great deal of nonsense was written as to the vandalism of the English; and the minds of certain people were so much inflamed by the

1 Weigall: 'A Report on the Antiquities of Lower Nubia.' (Department of Antiquities, Cairo, 1907.)

controversy that many regrettable words were spoken. The Department of Antiquities was much criticised for having approved the scheme, though it was more generally declared that the wishes of that Department had not been consulted, which was wholly untrue. These strictures are pronounced on all sides at the present day, in spite of the very significant silence and imperturbation (not to say supination) of Egyptologists, and it may therefore be as well to put the matter plainly before the reader, since the opinion of the person who is in charge of the ruins in question, has, whether right or wrong, a sort of interest attached to it.

In dealing with a question of this kind one has to clear from the brain the fumes of unbalanced thought and to behold all things with a level head. Strong wine is one of the lesser causes of insobriety, and there is often more damage done by intemperance of thought in matters of criticism than there is by actions committed under the influence of other forms of immoderation. We are agreed that it is a sad spectacle which is to be observed in the Old Kent Road on a Saturday night, when the legs of half the pedestrians appear to have lost their cunning. We say in disgust that these people are intoxicated. What, then, have we to say regarding those persons whose brains are unbalanced by immoderate habits of thought, who are suffering from that primary kind of intoxication which the dictionary tells us is simply a condition of the mind wherein clear judgment is obscured? There is sometimes a debauchery in the reasoning faculties of the polite which sends their opinions rollicking on their way just as drink will send a man staggering up the highroad. Temperance and sobriety are virtues which in their relation to thought have a greater value than they possess in any other regard; and we stand in more urgent need of missionaries to preach to us sobriety of opinion, a sort of critical teetotalism, than ever a drunkard stood in want of a pledge.

This case of Philae and the Lower Nubian temples illustrates my meaning. On the one hand there are those who tell us that the island temple, far from being damaged by its flooding, is benefited thereby; and on the other hand there are persons who urge that the engineers concerned in the making of the reservoir should be tarred and feathered to a man. Both these views are distorted and intemperate. Let us endeavour to straighten up our opinions, to walk them soberly and decorously before us in an atmosphere of propriety.

It will be agreed by all those who know Egypt that a great dam was necessary, and it will be admitted that no reach of the Nile below Wady Halfa could be converted into a reservoir with so little detriment to *modern* interests as that of Lower Nubia. Here there were very few cultivated fields to be inundated and a very small number of people to be dislodged. There were, however, these important ruins which would be flooded by such a reservoir, and the engineers therefore made a most serious attempt to find some other site for the building. A careful study of the Nile valley showed that the present site of the dam was the only spot at which a building of this kind could be set up without immensely increasing the cost of erection and greatly adding to the general difficulties and the possible dangers of the undertaking. The engineers had, therefore, to ask themselves whether the damage to the temples weighed against these considerations, whether it was right or not to expend the extra sum from the taxes. The answer was plain enough. They were of opinion that the temples would not be appreciably damaged by their flooding. They argued, very justly, that the buildings would be under water for only five months in each year, and for seven months the ruins would appear to be precisely as they always had been. It was not necessary, then, to state the loss of money and the added inconveniences on the one hand against the total loss of the temples on the other. It was simply needful to ask whether the temporary and apparently harmless inundation of the ruins each year was worth avoiding at the cost of several millions of precious Government money; and, looking at it purely from an administrative point of view, remembering that public money had to be economised and inextravagantly dealt with, I do not see that the answer given was in any way outrageous. Philae and the other temples were not to be harmed:

they were but to be closed to the public, so to speak, for the winter months.

PL. XXV. The island and temples of Philæ when the reservoir is empty.
*[Photo by R. Glendinning.]*

This view of the question is not based upon any error. In regard to the possible destruction of Philae by the force of the water, Mr Somers Clarke, F.S.A., whose name is known all over the world in connection with his work at St Paul's Cathedral and elsewhere, states definitely[1] that he is convinced that the temples will not be overthrown by the flood, and his opinion is shared by all those who have studied the matter carefully. Of course it is possible that, in spite of all the works of consolidation which have been effected, some cracks may appear; but during the months when the temple is out of water each year, these may be repaired. I cannot see that there is the least danger of an extensive collapse of the buildings;

1 Proc. Soc. Antiq., April 20, 1898.

but should this occur, the entire temple will have to be removed and set up elsewhere. Each summer and autumn when the water goes down and the buildings once more stand as they did in the days of the Ptolemies and Romans, we shall have ample time and opportunity to discuss the situation and to take all proper steps for the safeguarding of the temples against further damage; and even were we to be confronted by a mass of fallen ruins, scattered pell-mell over the island by the power of the water, I am convinced that every block could be replaced before the flood rose again. The temple of Maharraka was entirely rebuilt in three or four weeks.

Now, as to the effect of the water upon the reliefs and inscriptions with which the walls of the temples at Philae are covered. In June 1905 I reported[1] that a slight disintegration of the surface of the stone was noticeable, and that the sharp lines of the hieroglyphs had become somewhat blurred. This is due to the action of the salts in the sandstone; but these salts have now disappeared, and the disintegration will not continue. The Report on the Temples of Philae, issued by the Ministry of Public Works in 1908, makes this quite clear; and I may add that the proof of the statement is to be found at the many points on the Nile where there are the remains of quay walls dating from Pharaonic times. Many of these quays are constructed of inscribed blocks of a stone precisely similar in quality to that used at Philae; and although they have been submerged for many hundreds of years, the lines of the hieroglyphs are almost as sharp now as they ever were. The action of the water appears to have little effect upon sandstone, and it may thus be safely predicted that the reliefs and inscriptions at Philae will not suffer.

There still remain some traces of colour upon certain reliefs, and these will disappear. But archæologically the loss will be insignificant, and artistically it will not be much felt. With regard to the colour upon the capitals of the columns in the Hall of Isis, however, one must admit that its destruction would be a grave loss to us, and it is to be hoped that the

1 Les Annales du Service des Antiquites d'Egypte, vii. 1, p. 74.

capitals will be removed and replaced by dummies, or else most carefully copied in facsimile.

Such is the case of Philae when looked at from a practical point of view. Artistically and sentimentally, of course, one deeply regrets the flooding of the temple. Philae with its palms was a very charming sight, and although the island still looks very picturesque each year when the flood has receded and the ground is covered with grasses and vegetation, it will not again possess quite the magic that once caused it to be known as the "pearl of Egypt." But these are considerations which are to be taken into account with very great caution as standing against the interest of modern Egypt. If Philae were to be destroyed, one might, very properly, desire that modern interests should not receive sole consideration; but it is not to be destroyed, or even much damaged, and consequently the lover of Philae has but two objections to offer to the operations now proceeding: firstly, that the temples will be hidden from sight during a part of each year; and secondly, that water is an incongruous and unharmonious element to introduce into the sanctuaries of the gods.

Let us consider these two objections. As to the hiding of the temple under the water, we have to consider to what class of people the examination of the ruins is necessary. Archæologists, officials, residents, students, and all natives, are able to visit the place in the autumn, when the island stands high and dry, and the weather is not uncomfortably hot. Every person who desires to see Philae in its original condition can arrange to make his journey to Lower Nubia in the autumn or early winter. It is only the ordinary winter tourist who will find the ruins lost to view beneath the brown waters; and while his wishes are certainly to be consulted to some extent, there can be no question that the fortunes of the Egyptian farmers must receive the prior attention. And as to the incongruity of the introduction of the water into these sacred precincts, one may first remark that water stands each year in the temples of Karnak, Luxor, the Ramesseum, Shenhur, Esneh, and many another, introduced by the natural rise of the Nile, thus giving us a quieting familiarity with such a condition; and one may further point out that the presence of water in the buildings is not (speaking archæologically) more discordant than that of the palms and acacias which clustered around the ruins previous to the building of the dam, and gave Philae its peculiar charm. Both water and trees are out of place in a temple once swept and garnished, and it is only a habit of thought that makes the trees which grow in such ruins more congruous to the eye than water lapping around the pillars and taking the fair reflections of the stonework.

What remains, then, of the objections? Nothing, except an undefined sense of dismay that persists in spite of all arguments. There are few persons who will not feel this sorrow at the flooding of Philae, who will not groan inwardly as the water rises; and yet I cannot too emphatically repeat that there is no real cause for this apprehension and distress.

A great deal of damage has been done to the prestige of the archæologist by the ill-considered outbursts of those persons who have allowed this natural perturbation to have full sway in their minds. The man or woman who has protested the loudest has seldom been in a position even to offer an opinion. Thus every temperate thinker has come to feel a greater distaste for the propaganda of those persons who would have hindered the erection of the dam than for the actual effects of its erection. Vegetarians, Anti-Vivisectionists, Militant Suffragists, Little Englanders, and the like, have taught us to beware of the signs and tokens of the unbalanced mind; and it becomes the duty of every healthy person to fly from the contamination of their hysteria, even though the principles which lie at the base of their doctrines may not be entirely without reason. We must avoid hasty and violent judgment as we would the plague. No honest man will deny that the closing of Philae for half the year is anything but a very regrettable necessity; but it has come to this pass, that a self-respecting person will be very chary in admitting that he is not mightily well satisfied with the issue of the whole business.

Recently a poetic effusion has been published bewailing the "death" of Philae, and because the author is famous the world over for the charm of his writing, it has been read, and its lament has been echoed by a large number of persons. It is necessary to remind the reader, however, that because a man is a great artist it does not follow that he has a sober judgment. The outward appearance, and a disordered opinion on matters of everyday life, are often sufficient indication of this intemperance of mind which is so grave a human failing. A man and his art, of course, are not to be confused; and perhaps it is unfair to assess the art by the artist, but there are many persons who will understand my meaning when I suggest that it is extremely difficult to give serious attention to writers or speakers of a certain class. Philae is *not* dead. It may safely be said that the temples will last as long as the dam itself. Let us never forget that Past and Present walk hand in hand, and, as between friends, there must always be much "give and take." How many millions of pounds, I wonder, has been spent by the Government, from the revenues derived from the living Egyptians, for the excavation and preservation of the records of the past? Will the dead not make, in return, this sacrifice for the benefit of the striving farmers whose money has been used for the resuscitation of their history?

A great deal has been said regarding the destruction of the ancient inscriptions which are cut in such numbers upon the granite rocks in the region of the First Cataract, many of which are of great historical importance. Vast quantities of granite have been quarried for the building of the dam, and fears have been expressed that in the course of this work these graffiti may have been blasted into powder. It is necessary to say, therefore, that with the exception of one inscription which was damaged when the first quarrymen set to work upon the preliminary tests for suitable stone, not a single hieroglyph has been harmed. The present writer numbered all the inscriptions in white paint and marked out quarrying concessions, while several watchmen were set to guard these important relics. In this work, as in all else, the Department of Antiquities received the most generous assistance from the Department concerned with the building of the dam; and I should like to take this opportunity of saying that archæologists owe a far greater debt to the officials in charge of the various works at Aswan than they do to the bulk of their own fellow-workers. The desire to save every scrap of archæological information has been dominant in the minds of all concerned in the work throughout the whole undertaking.

Besides the temples of Philae there are several other ruins which will be flooded in part by the water when the heightening of the reservoir is completed. On the island of Bigeh, over against Philae, there is a little temple of no great historical value which will pass under water. The cemeteries on this island, and also on the mainland in this neighbourhood, have been completely excavated, and have yielded most important information. Farther up stream there stands the little temple of Dabôd. This has been repaired and strengthened, and will not come to any harm; while all the cemeteries in the vicinity, of course, have been cleared out. We next come to the fortress and quarries of Kertassi, which will be partly flooded. These have been put into good order, and there need be no fear of their being damaged. The temple of Tafeh, a few miles farther to the south, has also been safeguarded, and all the ancient graves have been excavated.

Next comes the great temple of Kalabsheh which, in 1907, when my report was made, was in a sorry state. The great hall was filled with the ruins of the fallen colonnade and its roof; the hypostyle hall was a mass of tumbled blocks over which the visitor was obliged to climb; and all the courts and chambers were heaped up with *débris*. Now, however, all this has been set to rights, and the temple stands once more in its glory. The water will flood the lower levels of the building each year for a few months, but there is no chance of a collapse taking place, and the only damage which is to be anticipated is the loss of the colour upon the reliefs in the inner chambers, and the washing away of some later Coptic paintings, already hardly distinguishable, in the first hall.

The temple is not very frequently visited, and it cannot be said that its closing for each winter will be keenly felt; and since it will certainly come to no harm under the gentle Nile, I do not see that its fate need cause any consternation. Let those who are able visit this fine ruin in the early months of winter, and they will be rewarded for their trouble by a view of a magnificent temple in what can only be described as apple-pie order. I venture to think that a building of this kind washed by the water is a more inspiring sight than a tumbled mass of ruins rising from amidst an encroaching jumble of native hovels.

Farther up the river stands the temple of Dendur. This will be partly inundated, though the main portion of the building stands above the highest level of the reservoir. Extensive repairs have been carried out here, and every grave in the vicinity has been examined. The fortress of Koshtamneh, which is made of mud-bricks, will be for the most part destroyed; but now that a complete record of this construction has been made, the loss is insignificant. Somewhat farther to the south stands the imposing temple of Dakkeh, the lower levels of which will be flooded. This temple has been most extensively patched up and strengthened, and no damage of any kind will be caused by its inundation. The vast cemeteries in the neighbourhood have all been excavated, and the remains of the town have been thoroughly examined. Still farther to the south stands the mud-brick fortress of Kubban, which, like Koshtamneh, will be partly destroyed; but the detailed excavations and records which have here been made will prevent any loss being felt by archæologists. Finally, the temple of Maharraka requires to be mentioned. This building in 1907 was a complete ruin, but it was carefully rebuilt, and now it is quite capable of withstanding the pressure of the water. From this point to the southern end of the new reservoir there are no temples below the new flood-level; and by the time that the water is raised every grave and other relic along the entire banks of the river will have been examined.

To complete these works it is proposed to erect a museum at Aswan wherein the antiquities discovered in Lower Nubia should be exhibited; and a permanent collection of objects illustrating the arts, crafts, and industries of Lower Nubia at all periods of its history, should be displayed. It is a question whether money will be found for the executing of this scheme; but there can be no doubt that a museum of this kind, situated at the virtual capital of Lower Nubia, would be a most valuable institution.

In 1907 the condition of the monuments of Lower Nubia was very bad. The temples already mentioned were in a most deplorable state; the cemeteries were being robbed, and there was no proper organisation for the protection of the ancient sites. There are, moreover, several temples above the level of high water, and these were also in a sad condition. Gerf Husen was both dirty and dilapidated; Wady Sabua was deeply buried in sand; Amada was falling to pieces; Derr was the receptacle for the refuse of the town; and even Abu Simbel itself was in a dangerous state. In my report I gave a gloomy picture indeed of the plight of the monuments. But now all this is changed. Sir Gaston Maspero made several personal visits to the country; every temple was set in order; many new watchmen were appointed; and today this territory may be said to be the "show" portion of this inspectorate. Now, it must be admitted that the happy change is due solely to the attention to which the country was subjected by reason of its flooding; and it is not the less true because it is paradoxical that the proposed submersion of certain temples has saved all the Lower Nubian monuments from rapid destruction at the hands of robbers, ignorant natives, and barbarous European visitors. What has been lost in Philae has been gained a thousand-fold in the repairing and safeguarding of the temples, and in the scientific excavation of the cemeteries farther to the south.

Here, then, is the sober fact of the matter. Are the English and Egyptian officials such vandals who have voted over a hundred thousand pounds for the safeguarding of the monuments of Lower Nubia? What country in the whole world has spent such vast sums of money upon the preservation of the relics of the Past as has Egypt during the last five-and-twenty years? The Government has treated the question throughout in a fair and generous manner; and those who rail at the officials will do well to consider seriously the remarks which I have dared to make upon the subject of temperate criticism.

# CHAPTER XII.

## ARCHÆOLOGY IN THE OPEN.

In this chapter I propose to state the case in favour of the archæologist who works abroad in the field, in contrast to him who studies at home in the museum, in the hope that others will follow the example of that scholar to whom this volume is dedicated, who does both.

I have said in a previous chapter that the archæologist is generally considered to be a kind of rag-and-bone man: one who, sitting all his life in a dusty room, shuns the touch of the wind and takes no pleasure in the vanities under the sun. Actually, this is not so very often a true description of him. The ease with which long journeys are now undertaken, the immunity from insult or peril which the traveller now enjoys, have made it possible for the archæologist to seek his information at its source in almost all the countries of the world; and he is not obliged, as was his grandfather, to take it at second-hand from the volumes of mediæval scholars. Moreover, the necessary collections of books of reference are now to be found in very diverse places; and thus it comes about that there are plenty of archæologists who are able to leave their own museums and studies for limited periods.

And as regards his supposed untidy habits, the phase of cleanliness which, like a purifying wind, descended suddenly upon the world in the second half of the nineteenth century, has penetrated even to libraries and museums, removing every speck of dust therefrom. The archæologist, when engaged in the sedentary side of his profession, lives nowadays in an atmosphere charged with the odours of furniture-polish and monkey-brand. A place less dusty than the Victoria and Albert Museum in South Kensington, or than the

Ashmolean Museum at Oxford, could not easily be imagined. The disgusting antiquarian of a past generation, with his matted locks and stained clothing, could but be ill at ease in such surroundings, and could claim no brotherhood with the majority of the present-day archæologists. Cobwebs are now taboo; and the misguided old man who dwelt amongst them is seldom to be found outside of caricature, save in the more remote corners of the land.

PL. XXVI. A relief representing Queen Tiy, from the tomb of Userhat at Thebes. This relief was stolen from the tomb, and found its way to the Brussels Museum, where it is shown in the damaged condition seen in Plate xxvii.
*[Photo by H. Carter.]*

The archæologist in these days, then, is not often confined permanently to his museum, though in many cases he remains there as much as possible; and still less often is he a person of objectionable appearance. The science is generally represented by two classes of scholar: the man who sits in the museum or library for the greater part of his life, and lives as though he would be worthy of the furniture-polish, and the man who works in the field for a part of the year and then lives as though he regarded the clean airs of heaven in even higher estimation. Thus, in arguing the case for the field-worker, as I propose here to do, there is no longer the easy target of the dusty antiquarian at which to hurl the javelin. One cannot merely urge a musty individual to come out into the open air: that would make an easy argument. One has to take aim at the less vulnerable person of the scholar who chooses to spend the greater part of his time in a smart gallery of exhibits or in a well-ordered and spotless library, and whose only fault is that he is too fond of those places. One may no longer tease him about his dusty surroundings; but I think it is possible to accuse him of setting a very bad example by his affection for "home comforts," and of causing indirectly no end of mischief. It is a fact that there are many Greek scholars who are so accustomed to read their texts in printed books that they could not make head nor tail of an original document written in a cursive Greek hand; and there are not a few students of Egyptian archæology who do not know the conditions and phenomena of the country sufficiently to prevent the occurrence of occasional "howlers" in the exposition of their theories.

There are three main arguments which may be set forward to induce Egyptologists to come as often as possible to Egypt, and to urge their students to do so, instead of educating the mind to the habit of working at home.

Firstly, the study of archæology in the open helps to train the young men in the path of health in which they should go. Work in the Egyptian desert, for example, is one of the most healthy and inspiring pursuits that could be imagined; and study in the shrines overlooking the Nile, where, as at Gebel Silsileh, one has to dive into the cool river and swim to the sun-scorched scene of one's work, is surely more invigorating than study in the atmosphere of the British Museum. A gallop up to the Tombs of the Kings puts a man in a readier mood for a morning's work than does a drive in an omnibus along Tottenham Court Road; and he will feel a keenness as he pulls out his note-book that he can never have experienced in his western city. There is, moreover, a certain amount of what is called "roughing it" to be endured by the archæologist in Egypt; and thus the body becomes toughened and prepared for any necessary spurt of work. To rough it in the open is the best medicine for tired heads, as it is the finest tonic for brains in a normal condition.

In parenthesis an explanation must be given of what is meant here by that much misunderstood condition of life which is generally known as "roughing it." A man who is accustomed to the services of two valets will believe that he is roughing it when he is left to put the diamond studs in his evening shirts with his own fingers; and a man who has tramped the roads all his life will hardly consider that he is roughing it when he is outlawed upon the unsheltered moors in late autumn. The degree of hardship to which I refer lies between these two extremes. The science of Egyptology does not demand from its devotees a performance of many extreme acts of discomfort; but, during the progress of active work, it does not afford many opportunities for luxurious self-indulgence, or for any slackness in the taking of exercise.

As a protest against the dilettante antiquarian (who is often as objectionable a character as the unwashed scholar) there are certain archæologists who wear the modern equivalent of a hair shirt, who walk abroad with pebbles in their shoes, and who speak of the sitting upon an easy-chair as a moral set-back. The strained and posed life which such savants lead is not to be regarded as a rough one; for there is constant luxury in the thought of their own toughness, and infinite comfort in the sense of superiority which they permit themselves to feel. It is not roughing it to feed from a bare board when a tablecloth adds insignificantly to the impedimenta of the camp: it is pretending to rough it. It is not roughing it to eat tinned food out of the tin when a plate costs a penny or two: it is either hypocrisy or slovenliness.

To rough it is to lead an exposed life under conditions which preclude the possibility of indulging in certain comforts which, in their place and at the right time, are enjoyed and appreciated. A man may well be said to rough it when he camps in the open, and dispenses with the luxuries of civilisation; when he pours a jug of water over himself instead of lying in ecstasy in an enamelled bath; eats a meal of two undefined courses instead of one of five or six; twangs a banjo to the moon instead of ravishing his ear with a sonata upon the grand piano; rolls himself in a blanket instead of sitting over the library fire; turns in at 9 P.M. and rises ere the sun has topped the hills instead of keeping late hours and lying abed; sleeps on the ground or upon a narrow camp-bed (which occasionally collapses) instead of sprawling at his ease in a four-poster.

A life of this kind cannot fail to be of benefit to the health; and, after all, the work of a healthy man is likely to be of greater value than that of one who is anæmic or out of condition. It is the first duty of a scholar to give attention to his muscles, for he, more than other men, has the opportunity to become enfeebled by indoor work. Few students can give sufficient time to physical exercise; but in Egypt the exercise is taken during the course of the work, and not an hour is wasted. The muscles harden and the health is ensured without the expending of a moment's thought upon the subject.

Archæology is too often considered to be the pursuit of weak-chested youths and eccentric old men: it is seldom regarded as a possible vocation for normal persons of sound health and balanced mind. An athletic and robust young man, clothed in the ordinary costume of a gentleman, will tell a new acquaintance that he is an Egyptologist, whereupon the latter will exclaim in surprise: "Not really?—you don't look like one." A kind of mystery surrounds the science. The layman supposes the antiquarian to be a very profound and erudite person, who has pored over his books since a baby, and has shunned those games and sports which generally make for a healthy constitution. The study of Egyptology is thought to require a depth of knowledge that places its students outside the limits of normal learning, and presupposes in them an unhealthy amount of schooling. This, of course, is absurd.

Nobody would expect an engineer who built bridges and dams, or a great military commander, to be a seedy individual with longish hair, pale face, and weak eyesight; and yet probably he has twice the brain capacity of the average archæologist. It is because the life of the antiquarian is, or is generally thought to be, unhealthy and sluggish that he is so universally regarded as a worm.

Some attempt should be made to rid the science of this forbidding aspect; and for this end students ought to do their best to make it possible for them to be regarded as ordinary, normal, healthy men. Let them discourage the popular belief that they are prodigies, freaks of mental expansion. Let their first desire be to show themselves good, useful, hardy, serviceable citizens or subjects, and they will do much to remove the stigma from their profession. Let them be acquainted with the feeling of a bat or racket in the hands, or a saddle between the knees; let them know the rough path over the mountains, or the diving-pool amongst the rocks, and their mentality will not be found to suffer. A winter's "roughing it" in the Theban necropolis or elsewhere would do much to banish the desire for perpetual residence at home in the west; and a season in Egypt would alter the point of view of the student more considerably than he could imagine. Moreover, the appearance of the scholar prancing about upon his fiery steed (even though it be but an Egyptian donkey) will help to dispel the current belief that he is incapable of physical exertion; and his reddened face rising, like the morning sun, above the rocks on some steep pathway over the Theban hills will give the passer-by cause to alter his opinion of those who profess and call themselves Egyptologists.

As a second argument a subject must be introduced which will be distasteful to a large number of archæologists. I refer to the narrow-minded policy of the curators of certain European and American museums, whose desire it is at all costs to place Egyptian and other eastern antiquities actually before the eyes of western students, in order that they and the public may have the entertainment of examining at home the wonders of lands which they make no effort to visit. I have no hesitation in saying that the craze for recklessly bringing away unique antiquities from Egypt to be exhibited in western museums for the satisfaction of the untravelled man, is the most pernicious bit of folly to be found in the whole broad realm of archæological misbehaviour.

A museum has three main justifications for its existence. In the first place, like a home for lost dogs, it is a repository for stray objects. No curator should endeavour to procure for his museum any antiquity which could be safely exhibited on its original site* and in its original position. He should receive only those stray objects which otherwise would be lost to sight, or those which would be in danger of destruction. The curator of a picture gallery is perfectly justified in purchasing any old master which is legitimately on sale; but he is not justified in obtaining a painting direct from the walls of a church where it has hung for centuries, and where it should still hang. In the same way a curator of a museum of antiquities should make it his first endeavour not so much to obtain objects direct from Egypt as to gather in those antiquities which are in the possession of private persons who cannot be expected to look after them with due care.

*Transcriber's note: Original text read "sight".

In the second place, a museum is a store-house for historical documents such as papyri and ostraca, and in this respect it is simply to be regarded as a kind of public library, capable of unlimited and perfectly legitimate expansion. Such objects are not often found by robbers in the tombs which they have violated, nor are they snatched from temples to which they belong. They are almost always found accidentally, and in a manner which precludes any possibility of their actual position having much significance. The immediate purchase, for example, by museum agents of the Tell el Amarna tablets—the correspondence of a great Pharaoh—which had been discovered by accident, and would perhaps have been destroyed, was most wise.

In the third place, a museum is a permanent exhibition for the instruction of the public, and for the enlightenment of students desirous of obtaining comparative knowledge in any one branch of their work, and for this purpose it should be well supplied not so much with original antiquities as with casts, facsimiles, models, and reproductions of all sorts.

To be a serviceable exhibition both for the student and the public a museum does not need to possess only original antiquities. On the contrary, as a repository for stray objects, a museum is not to be expected to have a complete series of original antiquities in any class, nor is it the business of the curator to attempt to fill up the gaps by purchase, except in special cases. To do so is to encourage the straying of other objects. The curator so often labours under the delusion that it is his first business to collect together as large a number as possible of valuable masterpieces. In reality that is a very secondary matter. His first business, if he is an Egyptologist, is to see that Egyptian masterpieces remain in Egypt so far as is practicable; and his next is to save what has irrevocably strayed from straying further. If the result of this policy is a poor collection, then he must devote so much the more time and money to obtaining facsimiles and reproductions. The keeper of a home for lost dogs does not search the city for a collie with red spots to complete his series of collies, or for a peculiarly elongated dachshund to head his procession of those animals. The fewer dogs he has got the better he is pleased, since this is an indication that a larger number are in safe keeping in their homes. The home of Egyptian antiquities is Egypt, a fact which will become more and more realised as travelling is facilitated.

But the curator generally has the insatiable appetite of the collector. The authorities of one museum bid vigorously against those of another at the auction which constantly goes on in the shops of the dealers in antiquities. They pay huge prices for original statues, vases, or sarcophagi: prices which would procure for them the finest series of casts or facsimiles, or would give them valuable additions to their legitimate collection of papyri. And what is it all for? It is not for the benefit of the general public, who could not tell the difference between a genuine antiquity and a forgery or reproduction, and who would be perfectly satisfied with the ordinary, miscellaneous collection of minor antiquities. It is not for that class of Egyptologist which endeavours to study Egyptian antiquities in Egypt. It is almost solely for the benefit of the student and scholar who cannot, or will not, go to Egypt. Soon it comes to be the curator's pride to observe that savants are hastening to his museum to make their studies. His civic conceit is tickled by the spectacle of Egyptologists travelling long distances to take notes in his metropolitan museum. He delights to be able to say that the student can study Egyptology in his well-ordered galleries as easily as he can in Egypt itself.

All this is as wrong-headed as it can be. While he is filling his museum he does not seem to understand that he is denuding every necropolis in Egypt. I will give one or two instances of the destruction wrought by western museums. I them at random from my memory.

In the year 1900 the then Inspector-General of Antiquities in Upper Egypt discovered a tomb at Thebes in which there was a beautiful relief sculptured on one of the walls, representing Queen Tiy. This he photographed (Plate XXVI.), and the tomb was once more buried. In 1908 I chanced upon this monument, and proposed to open it up as a "show place" for visitors; but alas!—the relief of the queen had disappeared, and only a gaping hole in the wall remained. It appears that robbers had entered the tomb at about the time of the change of inspectors; and, realising that this relief would make a valuable exhibit for some western museum, they had cut out of the wall as much as they could conveniently carry away—namely, the head and upper part of the figure of Tiy. The hieroglyphic inscription which was sculptured near the head was carefully erased, in case it should contain some reference to the name of the tomb from which they were taking the fragment; and over the face some false inscriptions were scribbled in Greek characters, so as to give the stone an unrecognisable appearance. In this condition it was conveyed to a dealer's shop, and it now forms one of the exhibits in the Royal Museum at Brussels. The photograph on Plate XXVII. shows the fragment as it appears after being cleaned.

PL. XXVII. A Relief representing Queen Tiy, from the tomb of Userhat, Thebes.—BRUSSELS MUSEUM.
(See PL. xxvi.)
*[Photo by T. Capart.]*

In the same museum, and in others also, there are fragments of beautiful sculpture hacked out of the walls of the famous tomb of Khaemhat at Thebes. In the British Museum there are large pieces of wall-paintings broken out of Theban tombs. The famous inscription in the tomb of Anena at Thebes, which was one of the most important texts of the early XVIIIth Dynasty, was smashed to pieces several years ago to be sold in small sections to museums; and the scholar to whom this volume is dedicated was instrumental in purchasing back for us eleven of the fragments, which have now been replaced in the tomb, and, with certain fragments in Europe, form the sole remnant of the once imposing stela. One of the most important scenes out of the famous reliefs of the Expedition to Pount, at Dêr el Bahri, found its way into the hands of the dealers, and was ultimately purchased by our museum in Cairo. The beautiful and important reliefs which decorated the tomb of Horemheb at Sakkâra, hacked out of the walls by robbers, are now exhibited in six different museums: London, Leyden, Vienna, Bologna, Alexandria, and Cairo. Of the two hundred tombs of the nobles now to be seen at Thebes, I cannot, at the moment, recall a single one which has not suffered in this manner at some time previous to the organisation of the present strict supervision.

The curators of western museums will argue that had they not purchased these fragments they would have fallen into the hands of less desirable owners. This is quite true, and, indeed, it forms the nearest approach to justification that can be discovered. Nevertheless, it has to be remembered that this purchasing of antiquities is the best stimulus to the robber, who is well aware that a market is always to be found for his stolen goods. It may seem difficult to censure the purchaser, for certainly the fragments were "stray" when the bargain was struck, and it is the business of the curator to collect stray antiquities. But why were they stray? Why were they ever cut from the walls of the Egyptian monuments? Assuredly because the robbers knew that museums would purchase them. If there had been no demand there would have been no supply.

To ask the curators to change their policy, and to purchase only those objects which are legitimately on sale, would, of course, be as futile as to ask the nations to disarm. The rivalry between museum and museum would alone prevent a cessation of this indiscriminate traffic. I can see only one way in which a more sane and moral attitude can be introduced, and that is by the development of the habit of visiting Egypt and of working upon archæological subjects in the shadow of the actual monuments. Only the person who is familiar with Egypt can know the cost of supplying the stay-at-home scholar with exhibits for his museums. Only one who has resided in Egypt can understand the fact that Egypt itself is the true museum for Egyptian antiquities. He alone can appreciate the work of the Egyptian Government in preserving the remains of ancient days.

The resident in Egypt, interested in archæology, comes to look with a kind of horror upon museums, and to feel extraordinary hostility to what may be called the museum spirit. He sees with his own eyes the half-destroyed tombs, which to the museum curator are things far off and not visualised. While the curator is blandly saying to his visitor: "See, I will now show you a beautiful fragment of sculpture from a distant and little-known Theban tomb," the white resident in Egypt, with black murder in his heart, is saying: "See, I will show you a beautiful tomb of which the best part of one wall is utterly destroyed that a fragment might be hacked out for a distant and little-known European museum."

To a resident in Europe, Egypt seems to be a strange and barbaric land, far, far away beyond the hills and seas; and her monuments are thought to be at the mercy of wild Bedwin Arabs. In the less recent travel books there is not a published drawing of a temple in the Nile valley but has its complement of Arab figures grouped in picturesque attitudes. Here a fire is being lit at the base of a column, and the black smoke curls upwards to destroy the paintings thereon; here a group of children sport upon the lap of a colossal statue; and here an Arab tethers his camel at the steps of the high altar. It is felt, thus, that the objects exhibited in European museums have been *rescued* from Egypt and recovered from a distant land. This is not so. They have been snatched from Egypt and lost to the country of their origin.

He who is well acquainted with Egypt knows that hundreds of watchmen, and a small army of inspectors, engineers, draughtsmen, surveyors, and other officials now guard these monuments, that strong iron gates bar the doorways against unauthorised visitors, that hourly patrols pass from monument to monument, and that any damage done is punished by long terms of imprisonment; he knows that the Egyptian Government spends hundreds of thousands of pounds upon safeguarding the ancient remains; he is aware that the organisation of the Department of Antiquities is an extremely important branch of the Ministry of Public Works. He has seen the temples swept and garnished, the tombs lit with electric light, and the sanctuaries carefully rebuilt. He has spun out to the Pyramids in the electric tram or in a taxi-cab; has strolled in evening dress and opera hat through the halls of Karnak, after dinner at the hotel; and has rung up the Theban Necropolis on the telephone.

A few seasons' residence in Egypt shifts the point of view in a startling manner. No longer is the country either distant or insecure; and, realising this, the student becomes more balanced, and he sees both sides of the question with equal clearness. The archæologist may complain that it is too expensive a matter to come to Egypt. But why, then, are not the expenses of such a journey met by the various museums? A hundred pounds will pay for a student's winter in Egypt and his journey to and from that country. Such a sum is given readily enough for the purchase of an antiquity; but surely rightly-minded students are a better investment than wrongly-acquired antiquities.

It must now be pointed out, as a third argument, that an Egyptologist cannot study his subject properly unless he be thoroughly familiar with Egypt and the modern Egyptians.

A student who is accustomed to sit at home, working in his library or museum, and who has never resided in Egypt, or has but travelled for a short time in that country, may do extremely useful work in one way and another, but that work will not be faultless. It will be, as it were, lop-sided; it will be coloured with hues of the west, unknown to the land of the Pharaohs and antithetical thereto. A London architect may design an apparently charming villa for a client in Jerusalem, but unless he knows by actual and prolonged experience the exigencies of the climate of Palestine, he will be liable to make a sad mess of his job. By bitter experience the military commanders learnt in South Africa that a plan of campaign prepared in England was of little use to them. The cricketer may play a very good game upon the home ground, but upon a foreign pitch the first straight ball will send his bails flying into the clear blue sky.

An archæologist who attempts to record the material relating to the manners and customs of the ancient Egyptians cannot complete his task, or even assure himself of the accuracy of his statements, unless he has studied the modern customs and has made himself acquainted with the permanent conditions of the country. The modern Egyptians, as has been pointed out in chapter ii. (page 28), are the same people as those who bowed the knee to Pharaoh, and many of their customs still survive. A student can no more hope to understand the story of Pharaonic times without an acquaintance with Egypt as she now is than a modern statesman can hope to understand his own times solely from a study of the past.

Nothing is more paralysing to a student of archæology than continuous book-work. A collection of hard facts is an extremely beneficial mental exercise, but the deductions drawn from such a collection should be regarded as an integral part of the work. The road-maker must also walk upon his road to the land whither it leads him; the shipbuilder must ride the seas in his vessel, though they be uncharted and unfathomed. Too often the professor will set his students to a compilation which leads them no farther than the final fair copy. They will be asked to make for him, with infinite labour, a list of the High Priests of Amon; but unless he has encouraged them to put such life into those figures that each one seems to step from the page to confront his recorder, unless the name of each calls to mind the very scenes amidst which he worshipped, then is the work uninspired and as deadening to the student as it is useful to the professor. A catalogue of ancient scarabs is required, let us suppose, and students are set to work upon it. They examine hundreds of specimens, they record the variations in design, they note the differences in the glaze or material. But can they picture the man who wore the scarab?—can they reconstruct in their minds the scene in the workshop wherein the scarab was made?—can they hear the song of the workmen or their laughter when the overseer was not nigh? In a word, does the scarab mean history to them, the history of a period, of a dynasty, of a craft? Assuredly not, unless the students know Egypt and the Egyptians, have heard their songs and their laughter, have watched their modern arts and crafts. Only then are they in a position to reconstruct the picture.

Theodore Roosevelt, in his Romanes lecture at Oxford, gave it as his opinion that the industrious collector of facts occupied an honourable but not an exalted position; and he added that the merely scientific historian must rest content with the honour, substantial, but not of the highest type, that belongs to him who gathers material which some time some master shall arise to use. Now every student should aim to be a master, to *use* the material which he has so laboriously collected; and though at the beginning of his career, and indeed throughout his life, the gathering of material is a most important part of his work, he should never compile solely for the sake of compilation, unless he be content to serve simply as a clerk of archæology.

An archæologist must be an historian. He must conjure up the past; he must play the Witch of Endor. His lists and indices, his catalogues and note-books, must be but the spells which he uses to invoke the dead. The spells have no potency until they are pronounced: the lists of the kings of Egypt have no more than an accidental value until they call before the curtain of the mind those monarchs themselves. It is the business of the archæologist to awake the dreaming dead: not to send the living to sleep. It is his business to make the stones tell their tale: not to petrify the listener. It is his business to put motion and commotion into the past that the present may see and hear: not to pin it down, spatchcocked, like a dead thing. In a word, the archæologist must be in command of that faculty which is known as the historic imagination, without which Dean Stanley was of opinion that the story of the past could not be told.

But how can that imagination be at once exerted and controlled, as it must needs be, unless the archæologist is so well acquainted with the conditions of the country about which he writes that his pictures of it can be said to be accurate? The student must allow himself to be saturated by the very waters of the Nile before he can permit himself to write of Egypt. He must know the modern Egyptians before he can construct his model of Pharaoh and his court.

In a recent London play dealing with ancient Egypt, the actor-manager exerted his historic imagination, in one scene, in so far as to introduce a *shadoof* or water-hoist, which was worked as a naturalistic side-action to the main incident. But, unfortunately, it was displayed upon a hillside where no water could ever have reached it; and thus the audience, all unconsciously, was confronted with the remarkable spectacle of a husbandman applying himself diligently to the task of ladelling thin air on to crops that grew upon barren sand. If only his imagination had been controlled by a knowledge of Egypt, the picture might have been both true and effective.

When the mummy of Akhnaton was discovered and was proved to be that of a man of twenty-eight years of age, many persons doubted the identification on the grounds that the king was known to have been married at the time when he came to the throne, seventeen years before his death,[1] and it was freely stated that a marriage at the age of ten or eleven was impossible and out of the question. Thus it actually remained for the writer to point out that the fact of the king's death occurring

1 Weigall: Life of Akhnaton, p. 56.

seventeen years after his marriage practically fixed his age at his decease at not much above twenty-eight years, so unlikely was it that his marriage would have been delayed beyond his eleventh year. Those who doubted the identification on such grounds were showing all too clearly that the manners and customs of the Egyptians of the nineteenth and twentieth centuries, so many of which have come down intact from olden times, were unknown to them.

Here we come to the root of the trouble. The Egyptologist who has not resided for some time in Egypt is inclined to allow his ideas regarding the ancient customs of the land to be influenced by his unconsciously-acquired knowledge of the habits of the west. Men do not marry before the age of eighteen or twenty in Europe: therefore they did not do so in Egypt. There are streams of water upon the mountains in Europe: therefore water may be hoisted upon the hillsides in Egypt. But is he blind that he sees not the great gulf fixed between the ways of the east and those of his accustomed west? It is of no value to science to record the life of Thutmosis III. with Napoleon as our model for it, nor to describe the daily life of the Pharaoh with the person of an English king before our mind's eye. Our European experience will not give us material for the imagination to work upon in dealing with Egypt. The setting for our Pharaonic pictures must be derived from Egypt alone; and no Egyptologist's work that is more than a simple compilation is of value unless the sunlight and the sandy glare of Egypt have burnt into his eyes, and have been reflected on to the pages under his pen.

The archæologist must possess the historic imagination, but it must be confined to its proper channels. It is impossible to exert this imagination without, as a consequence, a figure rising up before the mind partially furnished with the details of a personality and fully endowed with the broad character of an individual. The first lesson, thus, which we must learn is that of allowing no incongruity to appear in our figures. A king whose name has survived to us upon some monument becomes at once such a reality that the legends concerning him are apt to be accepted as so much fact. Like John Donne once* says—

> "Thou art so true, that thoughts of thee suffice
> To make dreams truth, and fables histories."

But only he who has resided in Egypt can judge how far the fables are to be regarded as having a nucleus of truth. In ancient history there can seldom be sufficient data at the Egyptologist's disposal with which to build up a complete figure; and his puppets must come upon the stage sadly deficient, as it were, in arms, legs, and apparel suitable to them, unless he knows from an experience of modern Egyptians how to restore them and to clothe them in good taste. The substance upon which the imagination works must be no less than a collective knowledge of the people of the nation in question. Rameses must be constructed from an acquaintance with many a Pasha of modern Egypt, and his Chief Butler must reflect the known characteristics of a hundred Beys and Effendis. Without such "padding" the figures will remain but names, and with names Egyptology is already overstocked.

It is remarkable to notice how little is known regarding the great personalities in history. Taking three characters at random: we know extremely little that is authentic regarding King Arthur; our knowledge of the actual history of Robin Hood is extremely meagre; and the precise historian would have to dismiss Cleopatra in a few paragraphs. But let the archæologist know so well the manners and customs of the period with which he is dealing that he will not, like the author of the stories of the Holy Grail, dress Arthur in the armour of the thirteenth century, nor fill the mind of Cleopatra with the thoughts of the Elizabethan poet; let him be so well trained in scientific cautiousness that he will not give unquestioned credence to the legends of the past; let him have sufficient knowledge of the nation to which his hero or heroine belonged to be able to fill up the lacunæ with a kind of collective appreciation and estimate of the national characteristics,—and I do not doubt that his interpretations will hold good till the end of all history.

The student to whom Egypt is not a living reality is handicapped in his labours more unfairly than is realised by him. Avoid Egypt, and though your brains be of vast capacity, though your eyes be never raised from your books, you will yet remain in many ways an ignoramus, liable to be corrected by the merest tourist in the Nile valley. But come with me to a Theban garden that I know, where, on some still evening, the dark palms are reflected in the placid Nile, and the acacias are mellowed by the last light of the sunset; where, in leafy bowers, the grapes cluster overhead, and the fig-tree is burdened with fruit. Beyond the broad sheet of the river rise those unchangeable hills which encompass the Valley of the Tombs of the Kings; and at their foot, dimly seen in the evening haze, sit the twin colossi, as they have sat since the days of Amenhotep the Magnificent. The stars begin to be seen through the leaves now that the daylight dies, and presently the Milky Way becomes apparent, stretching across the vault of the night, as when it was believed to be the Nile of the Heavens.

The owls hoot to one another through the garden; and at the edge of the alabaster tank wherein the dusk is mirrored, a frog croaks unseen amidst the lilies. Even so croaked he on this very ground in those days when, typifying eternity, he seemed to utter the endless refrain, "I am the resurrection, I am the resurrection," into the ears of men and maidens beneath these self-same stars.

And now a boat floats past, on its way to Karnak, silhouetted against the last-left light of the sky. There is music and song on board. The sound of the pipes is carried over the water and pulses to the ears, inflaming the imagination with the sorcery of its cadences and stirring the blood by its bold rhythm. The gentle breeze brings the scent of many flowers to the nostrils, and with these come drifting thoughts and undefined fancies, so that presently the busy considerations of the day are lulled and forgotten. The twilight seems to cloak the extent of the years, and in the gathering darkness the procession of the centuries is hidden. Yesterday and today are mingled together, and there is nothing to distinguish to the eye the one age from the other. An immortal, brought suddenly to the garden at this hour, could not say from direct observation whether he had descended from the clouds into the twentieth century before or the twentieth century after Christ; and the sound of the festal pipes in the passing boat would but serve to confuse him the more.

In such a garden as this the student will learn more Egyptology than he could assimilate in many an hour's study at home; for here his five senses play the student and Egypt herself is his teacher. While he may read in his books how this Pharaoh or that feasted o' nights in his palace beside the river, here, not in fallible imagination but in actual fact, he may see Nilus and the Libyan desert to which the royal eyes were turned, may smell the very perfume of the palace garden, and may hearken to the self-same sounds that lulled a king to sleep in Hundred-gated Thebes.

Not in the west, but only by the waters of the Nile will he learn how best to be an historian of ancient Egypt, and in what manner to make his studies of interest, as well as of technical value, to his readers, for he will here discover the great secret of his profession. Suddenly the veil will be lifted from his understanding, and he will become aware that Past and Present are so indissoluble as to be incapable of separate interpretation or single study. He will learn that there is no such thing as a distinct Past or a defined Present. "Yesterday this day's madness did prepare," and the affairs of bygone times must be interpreted in the light of recent events. The Past is alive today, and all the deeds of man in all the ages are living at this hour in offspring. There is no real death. The earthly grave will not hide, nor the mountain tomb imprison, the actions of the men of old Egypt, so consequent and fruitful are all human affairs. This is the knowledge which will make his work of lasting value; and nowhere save in Egypt can he acquire it. This, indeed, is the secret of the Sphinx; and only at the lips of the Sphinx itself can he learn it.

CPSIA information can be obtained
at www.ICGtesting.com
Printed in the USA
BVOW06s2144271117
501407BV00005B/124/P

9 781374 967922